This book is dedicated to the memory of
Donal Agnew and Brian Bloomer

ALL THE RISINGS

Kevin Kenna

CURRACH PRESS

DUBLIN

First published in 2016 by Currach Press

55A Spruce Avenue, Stillorgan Industrial Park

Blackrock, Co. Dublin

www.currach.ie

ISBN: 978-1-78218-855-1

Set in Adobe Kepler Std 10/14

Book design by Helene Pertl | Currach Press

Printed by ScandBook, Sweden

Definitions on p. xiii from *The Shorter Oxford English Dictionary on
Historical Principles*. London: Oxford University Press (1964).

CONTENTS

ACKNOWLEDGEMENTS

My thanks, firstly, go to my wife, Margaret, who was enthusiastic about this project from the start and who exercised great patience in correcting the early and later drafts of the book.

Once again, I'm greatly indebted to my very special friend, Listowel man Jim Mc Mahon, who examined the later versions of the manuscript and made many cogent and helpful suggestions on various aspects of the book.

Also, I am very grateful to the staff of the National Library of Ireland, especially to Berni Metcalfe, Keith Murphy, Nora Thornton and Glenn Dunne. Thank you to Sinéad Farrelly of the National Gallery of Ireland who was particularly helpful.

The cooperation of Niall Bergin and Ben Delaney of the Office of Public Works at Kilmainham Gaol was much appreciated, as was that of Helen Rogers of the Carton House Hotel. Through the kind cooperation of Una Keogh, Castledermot Parish Secretary, I was able to make contact with historian Eamon Kane of that town, who provided me with very valuable information. Thanks are also due to Stephen Day of Armagh Public Library and of the beautifully restored No. 5 Vicars' Hill, who was very generous with his time and information. I say a special thank you to my old friend Seán Mallin, grandson of the 1916 leader Michael Mallin, for his help and advice.

I pay tribute to the various authors listed in the reference section at the back of the book, whose works were invaluable to me in the writing of this book.

To Fearghal O'Boyle, the Managing Director of Currach Press and his team, Leeann Gallagher, Shane Mc Coy, Patrick O'Donoghue, Michael Brennan, Ellen Monnelly and Helene Pertl, I am very grateful. Their friendly and professional expertise was second to none and the experience of working with them was thoroughly enjoyable from my perspective.

Kevin (Caoimhín) Kenna, Dublin, January 2016

FOREWORD

Compared to the history of other newer countries, the Irish story is a long one. Trace elements of those mysterious people who built Newgrange many thousands of years ago are to be found in our DNA. So also are those from the Vikings and the Normans and they date from 'only' a thousand years ago. All over Ireland – in place names, in language, in story and in song – are the events or incidents in our history reflected. One such incident is that concerning the name of a small village called 'Clonoulty' in County Tipperary, where several surnames of northern origin are to be found: O'Neills, O'Donnells, Dohertys etc. To the locals they have been accepted as part of the northern population, but the key is in the name of the village: it means in Gaelic 'the Ulster people', and they settled there after the Battle of Kinsale in 1601. Ireland is replete with such historical fossils.

Of late, much of our history has been consigned to dusty rooms, the media preferring in the digital age to dwell on matters of modern shallowness. Ballads recounting the heroes of old – Robert Emmet, Henry Joy Mc Cracken, Kelly the Boy from Killane, The Bold Fenian Men – are never sung now. In my youth they were commonplace. An oral tradition which kept them alive when there was no TV has become almost extinct. It would not be so worrying if there was not a suspicion that this erasure was a conscious one.

How refreshing, therefore, on the eve of the centenary celebrations of the Easter Rising of 1916, that Caoimhín Kenna should keep our memory jogged of those attempts over a thousand years to keep a flame alive despite adversities of many a kind. Such a lengthy perspective gives balance to the narrow political narrative that we have become accustomed to. I do hope that this book will be appreciated by young and old, and particularly by visitors from abroad, who will be introduced to Ireland's long story in a digestible form.

Jim Mc Mahon, Killarney, June 2015

INTRODUCTION

In every generation the Irish people have asserted their right to
national freedom and sovereignty.

— Proclamation to the People of Ireland, Dublin 1916

The aim of this book is to record the principal occasions in Ireland's
history when resistance was made to foreign rule. I have endeavoured,
in particular, to set down the corresponding historical accounts in a
fashion that is easily digestible. Consequently, where appropriate, I
have avoided undue detail.

Each discrete chapter has been devoted to an individual rising
within the prescribed definitions. Chapter 1 concerns the famous
'Battle of Clontarf' and, in a sense, stands alone in being uniquely to do
with the impact of the arrival of the Vikings in Ireland. Chapters 2 and
3 are linked to each other by the proximity of the time lapse between
them, culminating in the Battle of Kinsale (1601) and the Flight of
the Earls in the first case and the subsequent failed 1641 rising in the
latter case. Chapter 4 deals with the Battle of the Boyne and one can
contend in this case too that it 'stands alone' in that the native Irish
placed their hopes for a better life in an English King, namely James
II only to discover, too late, that the King's real interests lay not in
Ireland but in the wider English and Continental arenas. The remaining chapters (5 to 9) deal with risings that occur fairly close to one
another in terms of time and are bonded together in a spirit of nationalism. The final chapter deals with the Easter Rising of 1916. When
these last chapters are viewed in sequence it could be argued that
the 1916 Rising, although surprising to many at the time, seems in
hindsight to be an almost inevitable consequence of our long history.

In summary, this book is an outline record of some of the critical
eras in Ireland's past and the order in which these events took place.

Kevin (Caoimhín) Kenna

MAP OF MODERN DAY IRELAND

Map by KMDESIGN.

ULSTER (9)

Derry, Antrim, Tyrone, Down, Fermanagh, Armagh (these counties constitute Northern Ireland), Donegal, Cavan and Monaghan (these counties, with those listed following, are in the Republic of Ireland)

LEINSTER (12)

Louth, Meath, Westmeath, Dublin, Longford, Offaly, Kildare, Laois, Wexford, Wicklow, Kilkenny, Carlow

CONNAUGHT (5)

Sligo, Leitrim, Roscommon, Mayo, Galway

MUNSTER (6)

Clare, Limerick, Kerry, Cork, Tipperary, Waterford

DEFINITIONS

Rising

  The act of taking up arms or engaging in some hostile action; an insurrection or revolt.

Uprising

  An insurrection; a popular rising.

Insurrection

  The action of rising in arms or open resistance against established authority or government restraint.

Rebellion

  Organised armed resistance to the ruler or government of one's country; insurrection; revolt.

Revolt

  An instance on the part of subjects or subordinates of casting off allegiance or obedience to their rulers or superiors; an insurrection.

PREFACE

The oldest human remains found in Ireland are dated from about 7,000
BC. The first Irish people were a Mesolithic (Middle Stone Age) race,
probably arriving from Europe via northern Britain. A second group
arrived around 3,700 BC during the Neolithic (users of flint) period.
With this wave of arrivals came also advances in modes of living, pro-
gressing from 'fishing and hunting' agriculture to the importation of
domesticated cattle, sheep, goats and cereals. It was during the Neolithic era, too, that passage cairns/tombs, such as Newgrange, were
built. The Firbolg and the Tuatha Dé Danann were examples of the
legendary tribes that inhabited Ireland during this period.

Newgrange passage grave, entrance to the burial chamber, County Meath.

Newgrange passage grave, County Meath, is one of a number of prehistoric constructions on this site. It dates from about the year 3,200 BC. It has a winter solar alignment which lights up the inner chamber on 21 December each year. Being approximately 5,200 years old, it predates Stonehenge in England and the Egyptian pyramids.

The Celts came to Ireland about 350 BC. Celtic origins date from about 800 BC and their culture was known as that of Hallstatt from an upper Austrian site. This was in the early Iron Age period. The latter part of this age was the period of the greatest power of the Celts in Europe. This period was known as La Téne after a site in Switzerland. From central Europe, the Celts spread westwards into Spain, northwards into Britain and Ireland, southwards into Italy and east along the River Danube as far as Galatia (part of Turkey) in Asia Minor. One hypothesis regarding the origin of the Celts (Milesians) who first arrived in Ireland, based on the Book of Invasions, is that they came directly from Spain (Milesian = *Míl Espáine*. Latin: *Miles Hispaniae* = Soldiers of Spain).

These 'Gaelic' Celts conquered Ireland. Their language was of a different Celtic stream to that of the 'British' Celts who originated from France and the northern parts of the Rhine. Britain and Ireland were the last conquests by the Celts, meaning that today Ireland is the only extant Celtic nation state in the world.

In Ireland the period between 350 BC and about AD 800 was characterised in particular by the militaristic disposition of the Celts. Their control of the country manifested itself in the sectioning of the country between rival leaders. In about the year AD 100 the Celts formed a united kingdom of Connacht and Meath and this led to the creation of a central High Kingship that was to last for centuries.

Until the end of the tenth century the high kingship alternated between the northern and southern Uí Néill dynasties. In this case, 'southern' really meant more the 'central' part of Ireland. There were no legal rights attaching to the high kingship and it was, consequently, a weak institution which, until the impact of Brian Boru in about the year 1,000, carried little weight among the myriad of local kingdoms then prevailing in the country.

Ireland was significantly impacted upon by the arrival in the country of St Patrick in about AD 431. Patrick was preceded by Palladius, who was sent to Ireland by the Church in Rome. It was the impact of Patrick, however, that had the greatest effect on Ireland. During his lifetime, virtually the whole population was converted to Christianity. Even the Viking suppression in the ninth century could not eradicate Christianity from the Irish people.

By AD 800 the Celts in Ireland had achieved a definite form of civilisation. The only languages in use were Gaelic and, as a result of Church influence, Latin.

In his book entitled *A History of Ireland*, the author Edmund Curtis, referring to Ireland's natural features, made the following statement, which is relevant to this book:

> Its abundance of all that natural man desires has tempted many invaders, but no country has resisted invasion more successfully, for it is a difficult country to hold though easy to overrun, as the Normans found. The soft air and abundant rain, the extent and fertility of good soil, the food producing richness of Ireland all conspire to make life easy and enable the native race to recover quickly after the most devastating wars. Hence the high 'survival value' of the Irish people who have beaten invader after invader.

Chapter 1

THE BATTLE OF CLONTARF

AD 1014

PRINCIPAL CHARACTERS

BRIAN BORU
    King of Cashel (Munster), High King of Ireland, 1002–1014
MALACHY I (Máel Sechnaill I)
    King of Meath, High King of Ireland, 846–862
MALACHY II (Máel Sechnaill II)
    King of Meath, High King of Ireland, 980–1002 and 1014–1022
THORGEST
    Leader of the first Vikings in Ireland
OLAF (Amlaíb Cuarán)
    Viking King of Dublin, 945–947, 952–981
IVAR (Ívarr) 'BEINLAUS'
    Viking
SITRIC UA ÍMAIR
    Viking
SITRIC SILKENBEARD
    Viking/King of Dublin
MATHGAMAIN MAC CEINNÉTIG
    Brother of Brian Boru
GORMFLAITH
    Wife, in turn, of Olaf, Malachy II and Brian Boru
MAELMORA (Máelmórda)
    Brother of Gormflaith
DONNCHADH
    Son of Brian Boru
MURCHAD
    Son of Brian Boru
FLAITHBERTACH UA NÉILL
    Leader of Northern O'Néill Sept of Cenél nEógain
SIGURD HLODVISSON
    Viking Jarl (Earl) of Orkney
BRODIR OF ISLE OF MAN
    Viking Slayer of Brian Boru

BACKGROUND

In about the year AD 800 invaders from Scandinavia landed in Iceland and then made their way to the Scottish Isles, especially the Orkney Islands, the Shetland Islands and later, the Hebrides. These first adventurers were Norwegian. The Vikings who invaded mainland Britain were of Danish origin. There appears to be a difference of opinion among historians as to whether the origin of Vikings who came to Ireland was Norwegian or Danish. For convenience the simple nomenclature 'Viking' is used in this book. What can be stated for certain is that none of the arrivals hailed from Sweden, as those originating from that country engaged themselves elsewhere in Europe.

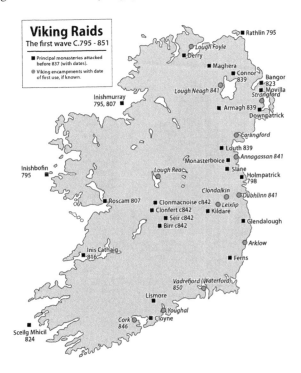

Map showing Viking Raids c. 795–851. Note: Weisfjord (Wexford) and Limerick were also founded by the Vikings, but after the period covered by this map. Map by KMDESIGN based on data compiled by Wesley Johnston.

First Vikings in Ireland

The first principal leader of the Vikings in Ireland was named Turgesius, or in Norse, Thorgest. His ships made their way up the River Shannon in the year 831 into Lough Ree and, in the north, through the River Bann into Lough Neagh. The strength of his forces resulted in his commanding the kingdoms of Ulster, Connacht and Meath.

The Vikings had a devastating impact wherever they arrived. They concentrated their attacks especially on thriving abbeys and churches because of their religious treasures and the wealth of their adjoining lands. They destroyed local art and books of learning and took slaves. The Annals of Ulster refer to early incursions of the Vikings into religious centres in Armagh, Bangor (County Down), Clonmacnoise (County Offaly) and Toomgraney or Tuamgraney (County Clare) as early as 794.

Clonmacnoise, monastic city. Founded in AD 545 by St Ciarán. It was plundered eight times by the Vikings and on a multitude of occasions by Irish and English raiders.

Entrance to the cathedral at Clonmacnoise. Rory O'Connor, the last High King of Ireland (1166–1198), was buried near the altar.

THE DEAD AT CLONMACNOISE
Thomas W. Rolleston
– Excerpt –

In a quiet water'd land, a land of roses,
Stands Saint Kieran's city fair,
And the warriors of Erin in their famous generations
Slumber there.

There beneath the dewy hillside sleep the noblest
Of the clan of Conn,
Each below his stone with name in branching Ogham
And the sacred knot thereon.

There they laid to rest the seven Kings of Tara,
There the sons of Cairbre sleep–
Battle-banners of the Gael that in Kieran's plain of crosses,
Now their final hosting keep.

There were Viking attacks also in the Skerries (County Dublin) area in 797, specifically on Church Island or Innispatrick, so called because St Patrick was thought to have been there in 432. To Thorgest, however, goes the credit for establishing Dublin (*Dubh Linn* – 'Black Pool'). Previously this area had been merely a crossing place on the River Liffey and known to the Irish as Áth Cliath (Ford of the Hurdles). The Vikings were also said to have attacked Skellig Michael off the Dingle Peninsula, County Kerry, in about the year 824.

After ruling for a period of fourteen years, Thorgest ended up in a watery grave in Lough Ennel (County Westmeath) in 845, courtesy of Malachy I (Máel Sechnaill I), King of Meath. Although the Irish otherwise suffered a number of defeats, they soon began to enjoy a measure of success against the invaders.

Battle of Sciath Nechtain, AD 848

Malachy I was a member of the powerful northern Uí Néill clan. The clan held sway also over Meath and assumed automatic entitlement to inherit the High Kingship of Ireland.

In 848, Malachy, who two years earlier had become High King (Árd Rí) of Ireland, gained a significant victory over the Vikings at Sciath Nechtain, near Castledermot, in County Kildare. (However, according to the Annals of Ulster, the victors were Ólchobor, King of Munster and Lorcán, King of Leinster.) But, in 852 the Vikings, under the leadership of Olaf the White and Ivar (Ívarr) 'Beinlaus', arrived in Dublin Bay and proceeded to fortify the area where Dublin Castle now stands. Malachy I died in 862 and there followed a period of intermingling and intermarrying between the invaders and the local population. This period of relative calm was also, at least partially, the result of the need by the Vikings to deal with the significant resistance to their presence in Britain by Alfred the Great.

Skenagun, Castledermot, County Kildare, the location of the Battle of Sciath Nechtain, ad 848.

Burial place of a Viking warrior, Cemetery of St James' Church, Castledermot, County Kildare. This is the only known Viking grave of its type ('hog back') in Ireland.

The Vikings Again

Ivar Beinlaus had already died in 873 but in 914 three of his grandsons, Ragnall, Sitric Ua Ímair (not to be confused with the later Sitric Silkenbeard) and Gofraid, landed in Waterford Harbour and commenced what was, in effect, a second phase of Viking incursions into Ireland in their endeavours to subdue the country. Three years after they had established a fortress at Waterford, Sitric sailed up the River Liffey and in 917 retook Dublin, which had been left undefended following the death of King Cerball in 909. Dublin had by now become a busy trading centre not only locally but also with other Viking-controlled areas in Wales, Scotland and English centres such as London, Chester and Bristol. Additionally, trading activities with Orkney and Shetland Islands linked trade right back to Norway.

Battle of Dublin, 919

Aed Findliath was High King from 862 to 879. He was very successful in opposing the Viking settlements in the north. His son, Niall

Glúndubh (Black Knee), leader of the powerful Uí Néill dynasty, succeeded him as High King. The occupation of Dublin by Sitric Ua Ímair acted as a spur to Glúndubh to march on Dublin in 919. His forces encountered those of Sitric at Kilmohavoc (Cill Mosamhóg) near the present Islandbridge in the Battle of Dublin, but the High King was killed and his forces defeated.

Further Viking Expansion

Limerick was next in line for occupation by the descendants of Ivar Beinlaus. This occurred in 920 when the city was added to the main strongholds of Dublin, Wexford, and Cork. Emanating from Ivar there emerged a line of Viking kings in the kingdoms of counties Dublin and Wicklow and reaching inland to Leixlip. These kings ruled with firmness from 944 onwards and in 977 they defeated the forces of the High King, Domnall. This resulted in all of County Meath from the Shannon to the east coast now falling under Viking control. Although Cashel itself now, too, fell to the invaders, there was no Viking impact west of the Shannon. High King Domnall died in 980.

Trade

The Vikings can be credited with founding what became Ireland's principal cities and with creating a trading tradition from which many local Irish people benefited. However, in carrying out their conquests, the Vikings created havoc against the Irish and a great deal of Irish culture, especially that comprising precious written works, was destroyed by them. At this stage, it could be said that the concept of Ireland as a 'Land of Saints and Scholars' – a title that was earned as a result of the bringing of Christianity to Ireland by St Patrick – had diminished.

The stranglehold of the Vikings was finally broken by two men: Brian Boru, who originally hailed from Dál gCais (in modern day County Clare), and Malachy II (Máel Sechnaill II), King of Meath.

Brian Boru

Brian Boru was born in about 942. His birthplace was thought to have been in Kincora (Ceann Coradh) – the present day Killaloe, County Clare. His family surname was Ceinnétig but the connotation 'Boru', meaning a cattle tax, was the one that took hold. There is a more likely explanation of his surname, which is that the name 'Boru' came from Bél Bóraime, a ring fort near where he lived at Killaloe.

Brian Boru sculpture, outside Chapel Royal in Dublin Castle.

When Brian was just a schoolboy his father, who was a minor king in Munster, was killed during a raid on the Dál gCais (Dalcassians) by Limerick Vikings. The Dál gCais was the adopted dynastic name taken from an earlier period and from which Brian Boru's forebears originated. It is likely that as a young boy Brian was sent for schooling to Inis Fallen on the Lakes of Killarney, a seat of Christian learning and popular with scholars since the time of the fall of the Roman Empire.

One of Brian's brothers, Latchna, succeeded his father but died in 953, and leadership was devolved on another of Brian's brothers, Mathgamain (Mahon) Mac Ceinnétig, who by 967 was described as King of Cashel (effectively covering all of Munster).

Ring Fort, Killaloe. Home base of Brian Boru, his family and his Dalcassian soldiers.

Battle of Sulcoit (or Solloghod), 968

In 963 Mathgamain had formed an alliance with Ivar, King of Limerick, presumably contrary to the wishes of Brian; later he changed his mind and rejoined Brian in the fight against the Leinster Vikings. In the Battle of Sulcoit (near Soloheadbeg in County Tipperary) in about 968 the brothers Brian and Mathgamain lured the Vikings into a thick forest area in which the Vikings were unable to implement their usual 'Wall of Shields' fighting tactics as they were unsuited to forest terrain. As a result, the Vikings suffered heavy losses.

Having overthrown Ivar's forces, the brothers marched on Limerick where they were again successful in routing the Viking opposition. Mathgamain ruled as King of Munster for eight years but was then killed by Ivar, or by someone appointed by him for the task. Brian, in turn, slew Ivar; thus began his own reign as King of Munster, which was to last from 976 to 1014. During this period he made challenges against Malachy II by raiding the kingdoms of Connacht and Leinster. He was not averse to availing himself of the services of Viking soldiers when it suited his military purposes to do so.

Battle of Tara, 980

Malachy II, a great-great-grandson of Malachy I, was born in 948 and was destined to outlive Brian Boru, not dying until 1022. He belonged to a Sept of the northern Uí Néill clan and was King of Meath. Later, in 980, he became High King. This elevation arose from his success in the Battle of Tara (the traditional seat of the High Kings of Ireland) in 980 against Viking opposition. One report stated that '5,000 Danes of Dublin were slain'. He then marched on Dublin where, in 981, he forced Olaf (Amlaíb Cuarán), King of Dublin, to surrender. Olaf had ruled Dublin since 952 and had done much to foster trade between the Vikings and the local Irish population. Possibly for reasons of consolidation, Malachy installed Sitric Silkenbeard, a son of Olaf, as King of Dublin.

An inevitable clash between Brian and Malachy ensued, but Brian had the upper hand in being able to send Viking ships from captured Limerick up the Shannon, thereby controlling both Connacht and Meath. Brian, as King of Munster, now moved to subdue Ossory (modern day Kilkenny and part of Laois) and Leinster, including Dublin. By 984 he achieved this and received the submission of Malachy. Finally, in 998, the Vikings having been largely broken, Brian and Malachy agreed to divide Ireland between themselves. Brian became head of the southern half (Munster and Leinster with Connacht previously secured) and including, now, Dublin. Malachy was allocated the northern half. In fact, Malachy retained power only in Meath as the north remained in the traditional control of the Uí Néill dynasties. However, Malachy probably felt that the agreement with Brian at least strengthened his hand vis-à-vis his northern relatives.

Gormflaith (Born about 955; Died about 1030)

Reference must now be made to a lady whose influence on this period of history was not inconsequential. This was Gormflaith. Gormflaith was said to have been born in Naas, County Kildare. She enjoyed a long and varied career, which was driven largely by her own personal interests with little regard for their impact on others. She became the wife of Olaf, but after his death in 981 she married Malachy, and later again she became wife of Brian. While still Malachy's wife, complications arose when he tired of her and 'dismissed' her. No doubt displeased with this, Gormflaith plotted to encourage her brother, Maelmora (Máelmórda), to enter a claim to the Kingdom of Leinster and to do so by uniting with Sitric, with the ultimate aim of breaking the bond between Malachy and Brian Boru.

Battle of Glenmama (Glenn Máma), 999

In 999 Brian responded to Maelmora's claim to Leinster by marching from Kincora in County Clare to Kildare, where he defeated the Sitric-led Viking/Leinster alliance at the Battle of Glenmama in the foothills of the Wicklow Mountains, near Ardclough in County Kildare, and triumphantly took Dublin. Later, however, Sitric made peace with Brian, was reinstalled in Dublin and, indeed, married Brian's daughter, Sláine. The resourceful Gormflaith, however, now cast her considerable spells on Brian, became his wife and bore him a son, named Donnchadh, to add to Brian's two other sons by his previous wife, named Mór. These were Murchad and Taig.

Brian had previously taken a second wife, Eachraidh. At some later stage Brian and Gormflaith divorced. A fourth wife of Brian's later appeared on the scene, Dubhchobhlaigh, who died in about 1008. The exact sequence in which he took his various wives is not clear.

THE BATTLE OF CLONTARF

The pact between Brian and Malachy was destined not to last and in 1002 Brian challenged Malachy to battle. Malachy, however, was unable to enlist the essential aid of the northern Uí Néill and succumbed. Brian Boru now became, finally, the High King of Ireland. To be fully effective in that role, however, there remained the difficult matter of subduing the northern Uí Néill.

There were three main kingdoms in the north: Cenél Conail, Cenél nEógain and the Ulaid Kingdom. Of these Cenél nEógain was the strongest and Ulaid the weakest. Ulaid fell to the other two which, in turn, were no match for Brian's forces, and the then leader of Cenél nEógain, Flaithbertach Ua Néill, was defeated in 1010. Brian's success was copper-fastened in 1011 when he overcame Cenél Conail.

Having been thwarted in previous attempts, Brian had consolidated his position in 1004 by undertaking a 'grand tour' of the country. In the course of this, the acceptance of his status by the Church in Ireland was demonstrated when he placed a gift of gold on the altar in the country's primary monastic centre in Armagh. By the same token, he accepted the supremacy of Armagh over the whole Church in Ireland. A short Latin text in the Book of Armagh refers to Brian Boru as *Imperator Scotorum* – 'Emperor of the Irish' (Scoti or Scotti was the generic term used by late Roman writers to describe Irish invaders of Roman Briton) – and may be indicative of his reputation on the Continent where such titles were used. (For example, the German Emperor Otto III, who died in 1002, was said to have been consecrated as 'August Emperor' by his cousin, Pope Gregory V.)

In the next period of relative calm in the country, Brian demonstrated his commitment to both Christianity and cultural matters generally by rebuilding ruined or damaged churches and founding new ones. He also arranged for the replacement of great books of learning that had been destroyed or damaged by the Vikings to be reintroduced from the Continent.

In summary, Brian was now claiming lordship of the whole Irish race – a unique moment in Irish history.

Map showing the main kingdoms of Ireland in 1014. Map by KMDESIGN based on data compiled by Wesley Johnston.

The following legend illustrates the aura of stability emanating from Brian's rule:

A young lady of exceeding beauty, undertook a journey from northern Ireland, adorned with jewels and a most costly dress. Testimony of the security there was in travelling, she carried a wand in her hand, with a gold ring of great value fixed on the top of it and arrived at a place called Tonn Cliodhna [Cliona's Wave] which lay in the southern part of the island ... no person attempted to injure her honour or to rob her of her ring that she carried openly on a stick, or strip her of her clothes which would have been valuable booty.

Thomas Moore's poem 'Rich and Rare Were the Gems She Wore' was composed based on this legend. An extract from the poem is given here:

Rich and rare were the gems she wore,
And a bright gold ring on her wand she bore;
But oh! her beauty was far beyond
Her sparkling gems or snow-white wand.

On she went, and her maiden smile
In safety lighted her round the Green Isle.
And blest for ever is she who relied
Upon Erin's honour, and Erin's pride!

But peace was not to last for long because Flaithbertach of the northern Cenél nEógain was not yet finally done for. In 1012 Brian sent Malachy to do battle with him. Although initially Malachy made successful incursions into Cenél nEógain, he suffered a humiliating loss a year later when Flaithbertach moved into Meath and defeated him.

The infamous Gormflaith may also have been at least partially to blame for the break in peace. While Malachy had been busy trying to keep control in the north, Gormflaith, still smarting from her repudiation by Malachy, and now too by Brian, urged Sitric and her brother Maelmora to react against what she described as their feudal and subordinate status. In order to achieve this she urged them to seek Viking support from outside Ireland.

Brian now determined, with Malachy's aid, to march his considerable army into Leinster in autumn of 1013. This he did, and remained in the vicinity of Dublin until the end of that year when they ran out of provisions. Meanwhile, his son, Murchad, was sent to do what damage he could to the enemy stationed in the Wicklow Mountains near Glendalough. When this did not bring about the desired result from Brian's perspective, he retired to Munster. This, however, was a temporary measure and Sitric, well aware of this, now received the sought-for additional Viking aid from overseas.

Sigurd Hlodvisson was the Jarl (Earl) of Orkney and he, with Brodir of Man, raised a large force of warriors to respond to Sitric's call for military help. It is thought that Sigurd's mother was possibly a Leinster princess and that, therefore, Sigurd had an additional interest or entitlement in making claims on Ireland. Apart from the enticement of gaining control of Ireland, both Sigurd and Brodir were promised (presumably separately) Gormflaith's hand in marriage by her son, Sitric.

By Easter week of 1014, the Viking force landed in Dublin where they were joined by Sitric and Maelmora, King of Leinster and his army.

Brian, meanwhile, had apparently been aware of the planned arrival of Vikings from overseas and had fortified a number of important sites along the Shannon in protection of Limerick and of his palace at Kincora. It is likely that Brian was very much aware of Viking successes in Britain and of the strong probability that, unless they were stopped now, Ireland was in danger of being overrun by yet another wave of Viking invaders. He drew together his forces, which were comprised of his Munster army and that of Connacht. His army was very large by Irish standards of the day and included troops from the Hiberno-Viking towns of Munster. His men were also well skilled in warfare and well armed. They camped at Clontarf, on the outskirts of Dublin, on the night of Holy Thursday, 1014.

Malachy, too, was camped in the area but, whether by agreement or otherwise, took no part in the battle that was to commence on the following morning – Good Friday. Indeed, it is possible that Malachy's non-participation in the battle was not 'by agreement'. In a pamphlet published in 1843 by a James Duffy, entitled 'Memoir of the Reign of Brian Boiroimhe', which admittedly seemed to give a very pro-Brian Boru slant on matters of the day, Malachy's absence from active involvement in the battle is described by the writer as follows: 'when to his [Brian's] great surprise, Malachy and the forces of Meath deserted their post, and retired with precipitation from the field of battle. This act of treachery and ingratitude in so considerable an ally as Malachy, at the first setting out of the action, animated the Danes.'

Malachy is further described by the same writer in the following terms:

> Maolseachluin [Malachy] was an indolent, inactive prince, addicted to pleasure and a love of ease and sacrificed the happiness of his country to his own private diversions; and the people who were immediately under his authority had contracted a servile habit of idleness from the example of the court and never disturbed themselves with opposing the inroads of the Danes.

The selection of an Easter date was undoubtedly because of Brian's Christianity and, perhaps, to convince himself that God was on his side. The fight could be described, consequently, as a battle of a Christian king versus heathen Viking opponents. Brian was said to have addressed his troops in the following terms:

> I am convinced that your valour and conduct will this day put an end to all the sufferings of your dear country, by a total defeat of these sacrilegious and merciless tyrants. And what

proves providential in our favour is, that we take full revenge of them for their constant acts of treachery and for the profanation of so many churches this Friday in Holy Week, on which Jesus Christ has suffered an ignominious death for our redemption, who will undoubtedly be present with us as a just avenger of his holy religion and laws.

Because of his age – he was seventy-three – Brian was too old to take an active part in the fighting; consequently, he delegated the command of his army to his son, Murchad. The Viking forces, under the command of Sigurd, sailed out of Dublin for Clontarf. They were probably smaller in number than those of Brian's but were heavily armed and well protected by body armour. Sitric, like Malachy, did not join in the battle that ensued. Instead he remained in Dublin, possibly to prevent its falling into Brian's hands.

The battle between the two sides commenced on Good Friday, 23 April 1014. A total of about 5,000 men were involved and the fighting lasted all day. One report, allegedly by Malachy, gave the following account of the battle:

I never beheld with my eyes, nor read in history an account of a sharper or bloodier fight than this memorable action; nor, if an angel from heaven would descend and relate the circumstances of it, could you without difficulty be induced to give credit to it; I withdrew with the troops under my command and was no otherwise concerned than as a spectator and stood at no greater distance than the breadth of a fallow field and a ditch. When both powerful armies engaged, and grappled in close fight, it was dreadful to behold how the swords glittered over their heads, being struck by the rays of the sun which gave them an appearance of a numerous flock of white seagulls flying in the air; the strokes were so mighty and the fury of the combatants so terrible, that great quantities of hair torn or cut off their heads by their sharp weapons, was driven

far off by the wind, and their spears and battle axes were so
encumbered with hair cemented together with clotted blood,
that it was scarce possible to clean or bring them to their
former brightness.

*Hugh Frazer's painting 'The Battle of Clontarf' showing Brian Boru's son, Murchad, in
combat with Sigurd, the Viking Jarl of Orkney on lower right side, and Brian Boru in his
tent on the left. Courtesy of Kildare Partners of Dublin.*

In the end Brian's forces were successful. The Viking soldiers were
forced to retreat, only to find that their escape route, via their boats
moored in the sea by Clontarf, was no longer available to them, the
boats having drifted away on a neap tide. Many of them were then
slaughtered on the beach.

In the battle Sigurd was killed, as was Brian's son Murchad and
many of his relatives. Brian, tradition has it, was praying in his tent
when he was recognised by the retreating Brodir who slew him on
the spot. Brian's success in the battle came at a high price. In addition to his family losses and his own demise, other supporters of Brian

also perished, including his erstwhile enemies the Éoganacht kings of Loch Léin (Killarney) and Fer Maige (Fermoy) together with the King of County Clare and a number of Connacht kings. By the same token almost the entire leadership of the Vikings/Leinster army, including Maelmora, lost their lives. The outcome, however, was clear: the Vikings had been defeated, and any feared further invasions from their overseas strongholds were now permanently halted. Nearly two centuries of Viking power in Ireland had come to an end.

Brian Boru's body was removed to Armagh and he was buried near the high altar at the north side of St Patrick's (now Church of Ireland) Cathedral. Brian's son Murchad, his grandson Turlough and others were thought to have been buried in a plot on the south side of the Cathedral, but this cannot be confirmed.

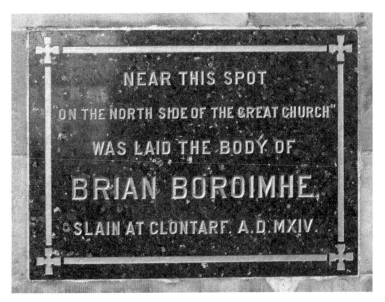

Plaque at front of St Patrick's Cathedral (Church of Ireland), Armagh.

KINCORA
James Clarence Mangan
– Excerpt –

Oh, where, Kincora! Is Brian the great?
And where is the beauty that once was thine?
Oh, where are the princes and nobles that sate
At the feast in thy halls, and drank the red wine
Where, oh, Kincora?

Oh, where, Kincora! Are thy valorous lords?
Oh, whither, thou Hospitable! Are they gone?
Oh, where are the Dalcassians of the golden swords?
And where are the warriors Brian led on?
Where, oh, Kincora? ...

Oh, dear are the images my memory calls up
Of Brian Boru! – how he never would miss
To give me at the banquet the first bright cup!
Ah! why did he heap on me honour like this ?
Why, oh Kincora?

Chapter 2

THE NINE YEARS' WAR

The Rising of Hugh O'Neill and Red Hugh O'Donnell

1594–1603

PRINCIPAL CHARACTERS

HUGH O'NEILL
  Earl of Tyrone
RED HUGH O'DONNELL
  Ruler of Tyrconnell (County Donegal)
RORY O'DONNELL
  Brother of Red Hugh O'Donnell
HENRY VIII OF ENGLAND
'SILKEN' THOMAS
  Earl of Kildare
ELIZABETH I OF ENGLAND
PHILIP II OF SPAIN
PHILIP III OF SPAIN
SIR HENRY BAGENAL
  Commander of English Forces in Ireland
SIR ROBERT DEVEREUX
  2nd Earl of Essex, Lord Lieutenant of Ireland
LORD MOUNTJOY
  Lord Deputy of Ireland
JAMES I OF ENGLAND
SIR HENRY DOCWRA
  Baron Docwra of Culmore, Leader of English troops in Ireland

BACKGROUND

In the period between the Battle of Clontarf in 1014 and the English/ Norman invasion of Ireland in 1169 the country had seen intermittent warfare between provincial kings. This was often to do with the position of the High Kingship of Ireland. Indeed it was a clash between Dermot Mac Murrough, King of Leinster, and the High King, Rory O'Connor, which set in motion the action by Mac Murrough to seek military aid from Norman Britain. The impact of the English/Normans can still be seen readily in Ireland today in the form of the ruins of castles and by surnames typically bearing the Norman prefix 'Fitz' (from the French *fils* for 'son of').

A period of territorial conquest and colonisation continued during the next 300 years or so, but was tempered to some extent by periodic Irish resistance and English distractions elsewhere in Europe.

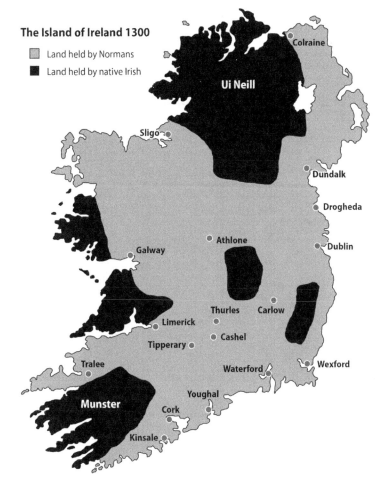

The Island of Ireland 1300

Land held by Normans

Land held by native Irish

Colraine

Ui Neill

Sligo

Dundalk

Drogheda

Athlone

Galway

Dublin

Thurles   Carlow

Limerick

Cashel

Tipperary

Tralee

Waterford   Wexford

Youghal

Munster

Cork

Kinsale

Map showing the impact of the English/Norman invasion in the year 1300. Map by KMDESIGN based on data compiled by Wesley Johnston.

When Henry VIII came to the English throne in 1509, almost three and a half centuries after the English/Norman invasion, his power in Ireland was largely confined to the area known as 'The Pale', which at that time comprised what today might be described as 'greater Dublin' together with parts of counties Wicklow and Louth.

The Island of Ireland 1450

■ Land held by native Irish
■ Land held by Anglo-Irish Lords
□ Land held by English King

Mac-Donnells

O'Donnell   O'Neill

Earldom of Ulster

Mayo Burkes   O'Rourke

Magennis

O'Reilly

O'Connor

O'Farrell

THE PALE

O'Flaherty   Burkes

Dempsey

Earldom of Kildare

O'Brien

Earldom of Ormond

Mac-Murrough

Earldom of Desmond

Wexford Lordship

Mac Carthy Mór

Map of Ireland c.1500. Map by KMDESIGN based on data compiled by Wesley Johnston.

Not only had Henry to contend with native Irish opposition to his reign, but also the not inconsiderable power of the 'Old English' settlers, who were content to enjoy their local independence and keep a certain distance between themselves and their king.

The term 'Old English' referred to descendants of settlers who came to Ireland during the English/Norman invasion. The term came into popular usage in the sixteenth and seventeenth centuries. The 'Old English' became assimilated into Irish society and were Catholic, as distinct from the later English Protestant Ascendancy class.

In addition, there were two other Continental considerations that were a cause of worry to Henry: the traditional rivalry of France to England; and the increasing importance and strength of the Kingdom of Spain. Henry was concerned that Ireland might be used by the French or the Spanish as a back door to attack England.

In 1534 Henry decided, therefore, that matters in Ireland needed to be brought in line. At that time even the House of Fitzgerald (Earls of Kildare), the King's strongest subjects in Ireland, was in open rebellion against him. It was in that same year that the then Earl of Kildare, Garret Óg Fitzgerald, was summoned to London and ended up being lodged in the Tower of London. His son, the flamboyant 'Silken Thomas' (so called because of his silken mode of dress), was left in charge. False rumours reached Dublin, however, that Garret Óg had been executed in London. (In fact, it was some time later when Garret Óg died in the Tower.) As a reaction to this, the young Silken Thomas revolted against the Crown and tried to take Dublin Castle, but was easily defeated. Silken Thomas and his five uncles were then also taken to the Tower and thence, in 1537, to Tyburn, where they were executed.

By this time, the Protestant Reformation had impacted on Ireland and the dissolution of monasteries had been implemented. Henry now decided that all land in Ireland would be taken over and, where he considered it appropriate, regranted to those upon whose loyalty he could rely. His success in this action of controlling the lands was limited; but when his daughter Elizabeth I came to the throne in 1558 she was ruthless in applying this policy. Her forces were largely comprised of Englishmen and not of the old English/Norman stock who, she considered, could no longer be trusted to deal with the 'barbarous' Irish. Although some resistance to Elizabeth's forces was shown by the Old English (with some local support), it was the native Gaelic-Irish population that bore the brunt of Elizabeth's demands. These demands resulted in brutal violence against her Irish foes, armed or unarmed, young or old.

Left: This pavement plaque, beside London's present day Marble Arch, marks the place, then known as Tyburn, where public executions were conducted on the 'Tyburn Tree' – a triangular wooden structure. Right: Marble Arch, London.

THE NINE YEARS' WAR

Towards the end of the sixteenth century Elizabethan armies firmly established English rule in Munster and Connacht. One of the principal leaders of opposition to Elizabeth in Ireland now came from Ulsterman Hugh O'Neill. O'Neill had spent eight years of his youth being raised in England. He was treated, nominally at least, as an Englishman and enjoyed access to Elizabeth's court. Later, in order to secure support for English rule in Ulster, the weakest of the four provinces as regards English control, Elizabeth helped O'Neill in his various disputes with other local chieftains and created him Earl of Tyrone. Notwithstanding this, Hugh's loyalties were divided between faithfulness to Elizabeth and an acute desire to be left unhindered and to his own devices in Ireland. In the end, he resolved to oppose Elizabeth and strike out for the independence of the Gaelic way of life.

In Hugh O'Neill Ireland had now found a man of real greatness – not only a soldier but a statesman too, with outstanding leadership qualities. O'Neill decided, therefore, to rise in arms against Elizabeth in his native Ulster. For this purpose he forged an alliance with fellow Ulster leader, (Red) Hugh O'Donnell, whose stronghold was concentrated especially in the west of the province. There followed a period of resistance against the Crown over the period 1594–1603, which became known as 'The Nine Years' War'.

Donegal Castle, Donegal town.

The castle of the O'Donnell clan was built in the fifteenth century, and underwent extensive additions and restoration in the seventeenth century by Englishman Sir Basil Brook. A significant portion of the right-hand side of the building is of the original building.

The Battle of the Ford of the Biscuits, 1594

In 1594 the first steps of resistance came about when Red Hugh O'Donnell and Hugh O'Neill's brother, Cormac Mac Baron O'Neill, defeated an English force at the 'Ford of the Biscuits' at the River Arney near Enniskillen, County Fermanagh. The reference to 'biscuits' came from the large amount of supplies left behind by the retreating English soldiers which included a consignment of biscuits intended to replenish stores at Enniskillen Castle, and which could be seen floating down the river.

This was just the start of the rising by the northern chiefs. By this time, too, the Irish cause had become a Catholic one and help was sought from Philip II of Spain and from the Pope. In an effort to entice Spain to provide aid, O'Neill and O'Donnell suggested that Philip send Albert VII, Archduke of Austria, to be King of Ireland. Albert was the son of the Holy Roman Emperor Maximilian II and Maria of Spain and, therefore, had a direct connection with the Spanish monarchy. This proposal, however, did not come to pass, although the possibility of aid coming from Spain was a primary reason for Elizabeth's continuing opposition to O'Neill.

Escapes

Prior to this, in 1587, Red Hugh O'Donnell had been captured near Lough Swilly in Donegal by English forces and incarcerated in Dublin Castle. In 1591 he made a remarkable escape from his prison, making his way on foot in foul wintry conditions over the Dublin/Wicklow Mountains. Exhaustion and freezing conditions forced him to rest overnight, short of his intended destination of Glenmalure in County Wicklow. His whereabouts was disclosed to the enemy by locals and he was returned to Dublin Castle.

On Christmas Eve of the following year, however, O'Donnell escaped again, this time with the aid, thought to be bribery, of Hugh O'Neill. Glenmalure was again to be his destination. Bad weather with very low winter temperatures meant, once again, a horrific journey to Glenmalure. One fellow escapee departed for the north and a second one, Art O'Neill, died on the way. O'Donnell was in very poor condition by the time he finally reached Glenmalure. This time he avoided recapture and, after he recovered somewhat, he returned to the north of the country.

Dublin Castle. Seat of British Administration in Ireland.

The Battle of Clontibret, 1595
In 1595, Hugh O'Neill successfully attacked an English force at Portmore, County Antrim. In that same year an English advance into Ulster under Sir Henry Bagenal (O'Neill's brother-in-law) was repulsed by O'Neill in the 'Battle of Clontibret' in County Monaghan. The battle lasted just two days. On the first day Bagenal's troops were ambushed en route while bringing supplies to Monaghan Castle. On their way back, to avoid further attacks, Bagenal took another route but was again ambushed by O'Neill's men. They took refuge at Ballymacowen and were eventually relieved when English reinforcements arrived from Newry. English losses were estimated to be in the region of 100–700, while the Irish losses were very much less.

In the following year, a truce was agreed with Elizabeth, but it did not last. The afforded 'waiting game' suited O'Neill as he was still expecting help from Philip II of Spain. He also lobbied other local leaders to rise in the Catholic cause. In 1597 the viceroy, Lord Brough, planned a threefold attack on Ulster. All three attacks, however, were repulsed, and a further truce agreed upon which lasted until the following year.

The Battle of Yellow Ford, 1598

The English, still under the command of Sir Henry Bagenal, now took the initiative and their forces (4,000 foot and 300 horse) met those of O'Neill and O'Donnell (comprising about 8,000 men) at Yellow Ford on the River Callan, possibly near where the river meets the River Blackwater, about two miles north of Armagh city. The Irish came away with a complete victory in which up to about 1,000 English troops were killed, while Irish losses were thought to be in the region of 300. A large number of English forces, possibly up to 1,000, deserted.

The River Blackwater at Blackwatertown, on the border between counties Armagh and Tyrone and close to the location of the Battle of the Yellow Ford.

After the Battle of Yellow Ford

Not for the last time in the course of Irish history, the victory roused local sentiment to the possibility of being able to obtain a measure of relief from the suppression of their overlords. By the end of that same year the Irish forces had grown in strength to about 30,000 men. At this stage O'Neill was largely in control also of Munster. This was due to the actions of O'Neill's commanders, Tyrell and Lacy, who raised a rebel army there. However, without artillery and other heavy weaponry, O'Neill had little chance of success against a fortified Leinster and Dublin in particular. Additionally, the anticipated help from Spain did not materialise. O'Neill and O'Donnell were awaiting the expected death of Elizabeth with the possible succession of a more sympathetic, supposedly Catholic, James of Scotland to the throne. Meanwhile, O'Neill's control in Munster waned.

In 1599 the Earl of Essex, Lord Lieutenant of Ireland, was sent by Elizabeth with an army of 16,000 to deal with the Irish. However, due to the Earl's poor tactics in attacks in Munster and south Leinster his army was reduced to only about 4,000. Contrary to Elizabeth's wishes Essex agreed a truce with O'Neill; the result was that he was quickly recalled by Her Majesty and executed. Elizabeth now appointed Lord Mountjoy to replace Essex and a new plan of action against the Irish was put in place. The new plan was to defeat the Irish by the imposition of famine. In the year 1600, Mountjoy's massacre of the troops of various garrisons and the destruction of crops brought Munster back under English control once again. Pressure on the north was spearheaded by Sir Henry Docwra who, in that same year, occupied Derry and managed to 'buy over' a number of northern chiefs including Sir Arthur O'Neill, Niall Garbh O'Donnell and Donal O'Cahan. His chief efforts were concentrated, therefore, in north-west Ulster.

The Battle of Kinsale, 1601

When Spanish aid finally landed (at the behest of the new king, Philip III) it was disappointingly small – only about 4,000 troops – and it had the signal disadvantage of landing in Kinsale, County Cork, at the opposite end of the country to where it was really needed, the north now being besieged by the Queen's troops. Consequently, O'Neill and O'Donnell had little option but to march their forces southwards to link up with the Spanish. Mountjoy was alert to the situation and arrived first at Kinsale to lay siege to the Spanish visitors and their local supporters.

O'Neill and O'Donnell arrived at Kinsale towards the end of 1601 and they, in turn, began to lay siege to the besiegers. The outcome of this stand-off was now critical for the future course of Irish history. O'Neill and O'Donnell were in a strong position militarily. Their forces numbered about 12,000 together with the besieged Spanish of 4,000 as against Mountjoy's army of only 6,500. The leader of the Spanish, Don Juan D'Aguila, pushed for a decisive battle, contrary to the wishes of O'Neill and O'Donnell. In any event, for reasons that are not clear, D'Aguila got his way and on 24 December 1601 battle commenced. Despite their numerical advantage the Irish/Spanish forces were defeated. No doubt motivated by shock and disappointment, O'Donnell fled to Spain where he died a year later.

O'Neill was forced to retire to his northern base. Mountjoy, however, continued to exert pressure on the north and in 1603, after a stubborn resistance together with other local chieftains, Rory O'Donnell, Red Hugh O'Donnell's brother and successor, surrendered to Mountjoy. Hugh now found that he, too, had no real alternative but to submit to Elizabeth and on 30 March 1603 he did so. A week previously, in fact, Elizabeth had died and it was necessary for O'Neill to make a fresh submission to the new King of England, James I.

O'Neill and Rory O'Donnell were summoned to London where they were received more kindly by King James than they would have been by Elizabeth. O'Neill was restored to his earldom of Tyrone while O'Donnell was made Earl of Tyrconnell (the area of today's Donegal, approximately). These titles, however, were largely nominal and both leaders were rendered powerless. They were forced to abandon their Irish titles and their armies and to submit to the Crown of England. The upshot was that Ulster, the last unconquered province of Ireland, was now under the control of English law and government and was ripe for the Plantation of Ulster which was to follow.

The old Brehon Laws on tenure were set aside and replaced by English landlordism and so the rising of Hugh O'Neill and Red Hugh

O'Donnell ended in failure. Notwithstanding this, by the end of Elizabeth's reign in 1603 the seeds of a new future resistance to English rule were sown. An indication of this was that, contrary to the firm position of the Protestant Church in England, which Elizabeth formally established and of which she was Supreme Governor, the Reformation of the Church in Ireland had failed and the Irish Church prevailed, remaining faithful to the Pope as its head and largely supported by the native Irish.

THE MARCH TO KINSALE
Aubrey De Vere
– Excerpt –

O'er many a river bridged with ice,
Through many a vale with snow-drifts dumb,
Past quaking fen and precipice
The Princes of the North are come!
Lo, these are they that, year by year,
Rolled back the tide of England's war;–
Rejoice, Kinsale! Thy help is near!
That wondrous winter march is o'er.
And thus they sang, 'To-morrow morn
'Our eyes shall rest upon the foe:
'Roll on, swift night, in silence borne,
'And blow, thou breeze of sunrise blow!'

The Flight of the Earls
In 1607 Hugh O'Neill and Rory O'Donnell (Red Hugh's brother) and about 100 supporters left Ireland for good in what became known as 'The Flight of the Earls'. They were prompted to leave their native land by the realisation that they were no longer masters of their own destiny. They were being harried by English officials who were applying English law in their territories and continually making the practice of their Catholic religion extremely difficult and costly. Their intended

destination was Spain, via the Spanish Netherlands, but they ended up in Rome. En route they were welcomed in Louvain at the Franciscan Irish College. Their aim was to elicit Catholic support on the Continent for their cause, but in this quest they were unsuccessful.

Rory O'Donnell died in Rome in 1608. Hugh O'Neill, The Great Earl, died in the year 1616, also in Rome, and was interred in the Church of San Pietro di Montorio beside Rory O'Donnell.

O'DONNELL ABU
M.J. Mc Cann
– Excerpt –

Princely O'Neill to our aid is advancing,
With many a chieftain and warrior clan,
A thousand proud steeds in his vanguard are prancing,
'Neath the borderers brave from the banks of the Bann;
Many a heart shall quail
Under its coat of mail;
Deeply the merciless foeman shall rue,
When on his ear shall ring,
Borne on the breeze's wing,
Tir-Conaill's dread war-cry – O'Donnell abu!

Sacred the cause that Clann-Conaill's defending,
The altars we kneel at and homes of our sires;
Ruthless the ruin the foe is extending,
Midnight is red with the plunderer's fires!
On with O'Donnell, then,
Fight the old fight again,
Sons of Tir-Conaill, all valiant and true
Make the false Saxon feel
Erin's avenging steel!
Strike for your country: O'Donnell abu!

— from *The Spirit of the Nation*, Dublin, 1927

Chapter 3

THE 1641 RISING

The Great Catholic/Gaelic Rising for the Return of the Lands

PRINCIPAL CHARACTERS

FELIM O'NEILL
Leader of the Ulster Irish and of the Rising

RORY O'MORE
Leader of the Rising

HUGH ÓG MAC MAHON
Leader of the Rising

CONOR MAGUIRE
Leader of the Rising

KING CHARLES I OF ENGLAND

JOHN BAPTIST RINUCCINI
Papal Nuncio to the Confederation of Kilkenny

GENERAL PRESTON
Commander of the Southern Forces of the Confederation of
Kilkenny

JAMES BUTLER, EARL OF ORMOND
Head of English Forces in Ireland

GENERAL MUNRO
Scottish Commander of the Parliamentarian Army in Ulster

OLIVER CROMWELL
Leader of the 'Republican' movement in England

GENERAL IRETON
Son-in-Law of Oliver Cromwell and Lord Lieutenant of Ireland

OWEN ROE (EOGHAN RUADH) O'NEILL
Commander of the Confederate forces in Ulster

THOMAS WENTWORTH, EARL OF STRAFFORD
Viceroy and Lord Deputy of Ireland

BACKGROUND

From the time of the Battle of Kinsale (1601) and The Flight of the
Earls (1607) onwards, a new order in Ireland had begun. The whole
of Ireland was now to be united as a kingdom under the English

monarchy. There was, however, a difficulty for the monarchy, namely how to reconcile a Catholic native population, born of oppression, with an Anglican government supported by an intolerant Protestant ascendancy whose position was fortified by continuing plantations?

The Brehon Laws and the Irish system of land tenure were now replaced by the rules of English landlordism. The Brehon Laws probably dated from Celtic times and survived until they were replaced by English common law. The earlier law was administered by Brehons, the successors to Celtic druids, whose role was akin to that of arbitrators. Brehon Law included recognition of divorce and equal rights. Under its law of succession (tanistry) the eldest son succeeded his father in almost all circumstances.

In 1606, James I had inserted into severe anti-Catholic laws a new oath of allegiance. Under these provisions Catholics could be considered as loyal men only if (1) they accepted James as lawful and rightful king and (2) they repudiated the right of the Pope to depose him. The oath had few takers among the native Irish. The same could be said of a royal proclamation, which had been issued in the previous year, and which ordered that all were to conform to 'that religion which is agreeable to God's word and is established by the laws of the Realm'.

Plantation of Ulster

In 1614, Sir George Carew, formerly President of Munster, sent a paper to King James in which he stated that Catholic religious feeling had brought together the native Irish and the 'Old English' (those who were descendants of settlers who arrived in Ireland after the English/ Norman invasion of the twelfth century) and that he could foresee a danger that they would rebel under the banner of religious liberty. Meanwhile, plantations continued. The allocation of land now also applied to Scottish planters who were, in the main, Presbyterian. There was now, too, a particular concentration on Ulster. The counties of Armagh, Cavan, Fermanagh, Tyrone, Derry and Donegal were declared property of the Crown and detailed plantation plans were instigated. The fulfilling of the original intention of forming totally non-Irish holdings was thwarted, however, because many new settlers were unable to entice fellow settlers to come and work for them. The Irish tenants who filled these gaps, understandably, remained resentful of having to work for those who had effectively stolen their land.

One of the most significant outcomes of the plantations concerned Derry. In London, there was a conglomerate of business companies which had long been established as 'The City of London'. This grouping, now comprising twelve companies, was granted all of the northern part of Derry; this resulted in their controlling the valuable forests and fisheries of the area. In return for payment of a small head rent, and the giving of an undertaking to accept only Scots and English as tenants, the City was granted freedom of the importation and exportation of all commodities. Thus was created the title 'Londonderry', which referred to the whole county and not only to the city. Today both the city and county are referred to as Derry by Nationalists, while Loyalists still declare it to be 'Londonderry'.

In the plantation process, some Irish did receive grants of land, but the mass of the population became merely tenants-at-will or labourers.

Notwithstanding the impact of the plantations, a Gaelic aristocracy remained in Ulster. This included Sir Henry Óg O'Neill, whose grandson, Felim O'Neill, was to lead the 1641 Rising. The upshot of the plantations was that most of Ulster became Protestant. The implementation of the plantations took place during a period of peace, due, no doubt, to the Irish being disarmed and to the existence of a large army of occupation which discouraged any resistance.

Further Plantations

The success of the Ulster plantation encouraged the implementation of further ones. From 1610 to the beginning of the reign of Charles I in 1625, the areas selected included north Wexford, south Carlow, parts of Wicklow, Longford, Leitrim and south Offaly. The old Gaelic order was, in this way, brought to an end and the masses were now, at best, mere leaseholders.

In 1588 Richard Boyle, a capable English businessman seeking his fortune, arrived in Munster. Although he had little by way of personal financial wealth, he hailed from a 'comfortable' family background and managed to acquire large tracts of land in the province. He tapped into the undeveloped economic wealth of the area and promoted the commercial development of forestry, fisheries, linen and other cloth weaving activities. He also promoted iron smelting with the help of his 'imported' settlers. He was created Earl of Cork in 1620. He later built a number of towns, such as Clonakilty, and was also credited with the development of Bandon. Boyle was actively anti-Catholic and ensured that the saying of Mass was banned. He was also instrumental in the destruction of monasteries. Envy of Boyle's commercial success provided him with numerous enemies, especially Viceroy Thomas Wentworth.

Boyle died in 1643, having lost all his lands as a result of the 1641 Rising. One of Boyle's sons was the Hon. Robert Boyle, who was the creator of Boyle's Law in Chemistry.

Despite the negative impact of the plantations from an Irish perspective, up to 1640 Catholic landowners and Old English landowners (the latter being considered by the authorities as the more important) held two thirds of the land. This fact, due in the main to there being insufficient numbers of the English/Scottish settlers available, made the impact of Catholics in political and religious matter relatively strong. In Ireland they were not barred from the House of Commons, as was the case in England. However, the Protestant majority in Dublin was 'managed' by the creation of an appropriate number of boroughs returning Protestant members. Additionally, the law debarred Catholics from the practice of the law, from running schools and from gaining university degrees. Intolerance of Catholics could also be discerned by a statement issued in 1627 by James Ussher, Protestant Archbishop of Armagh, in which he declared: 'The religion of the Papists is superstitious and heretical and Toleration is a grievous sin.'

Charles I

The reign of the newly crowned Charles I in 1625 held out hope to the Catholic population, or, at least, to the upper classes of them. This was because the King's wife was Catholic and his sympathy towards High Church practice made him inclined, it was thought, towards religious tolerance. The King needed to increase his revenue from Ireland and he considered that concessions on land and religion would be advisable for this purpose. What emerged was a decision that land titles held for sixty years back were to be valid against all claims of the Crown, and furthermore, that Catholics were to be allowed to practise at the Bar on the taking of a simple oath of allegiance to the King. In return for these 'Graces', recusants (Catholics who had to pay fines, suffer imprisonment, and/or property confiscations for refusing to attend Protestant church services) were to pay over £120,000 and a parliament was to be formed to confirm the agreement. The money was paid over but the King reneged on the deal.

The period that followed was characterised by the impact in Ireland of the viceroy, Sir Thomas Wentworth. He was created Lord Deputy of Ireland in 1632 and Lord Lieutenant in 1639, and created Earl of Strafford. In what was then a struggle between king and the English Parliament, Wentworth intended to get the Catholics on the side of the monarchy. He called a parliament in Dublin in 1634 and although it promised, once again, certain 'Graces', he dissolved it a year later and watered down the 'Graces', especially those regarding the confirmation of certain land titles. He then set about the plantation of Connacht and Clare, the west generally being still Gaelic and, as regards the landed classes, Norman. However, Wentworth didn't make any significant inroads in this regard. He did, however, successfully encourage industrial endeavour in the country and made those in control highly prosperous which, in turn, provided a significant surplus for the Crown.

Wentworth's time in Ireland was curtailed when the battle between King and Parliament moved in favour of the latter. By about this time it could be said that four distinct parties existed in Ireland as follows:

1. The Old Irish (Native Irish), whose aims were to restore the Catholic religion in the country and expel the English and their Scottish supporters from Ireland.
2. The Old English (Anglo Irish), who were *ad idem* with the native Irish as regards the Catholic religion but who wished to continue as loyal subjects of the King.
3. The Royalists, who wished to promote the interests of the King in every way and who sought to maintain the Protestant (Established) Church in Ireland.
4. The Parliamentarians, who were supported by the English Parliament and who opposed all religions apart from those of Puritans and Presbyterians.

THE 1641 RISING

In 1641, the Long Parliament in England (so named to distinguish it from the Short Parliament which lasted for only a short time) summoned Wentworth to London as a result of their receiving complaints from various aggrieved parties in Ireland, due partially to his oppressive endeavours to exact taxes and duties from the Old English. On his arrival, he was sent to the scaffold at the behest of the Parliament. The command of Dublin was now given to two Parliament men, Borlase and Parsons, both Lords Justices, whose disastrous rule and anti-Catholic resolve had the effect of driving Irish Roman Catholics, even those most loyal to the Crown, into rebellion. This may have been intentional on the part of both of them in the sense that a rebellion would result in more land confiscations which would be an embarrassment to the King.

A factor on the Irish side was that a general revolt in England against the monarchy provided food for thought to the Irish, who could foresee that their grievances, including religious ones, which had been ignored up to now, might also be redressed by force. There were two principal elements of the rising that was to follow, namely domestic and foreign. On the domestic front, a leader emerged in the form of Rory O'More (Ruaidhri Ó Mordha) of Laois, while on the foreign front, there were forces of Irish soldiers in the service of Spain, France and Austria, together with a cohort of Irish priests and friars around Europe which might be able to call on papal support.

Another important leader was Felim O'Neill – a member of the famous O'Neill dynasty. He was a great-grandson of Henry Mac Shane O'Neill, one of the O'Neills who remained in Ulster after The Flight of the Earls.

The rising was supported, too, by the Irish peasantry who were severely hit by a bad harvest in 1641 and by rising rents.

The plan of the rising, to be executed on 23 October 1641, was that Rory O'More and Felim O'Neill were to take Derry and other northern towns, while Hugh Óg Mac Mahon and Lord Conor Maguire were to seize Dublin Castle. Monaghan-born Mac Mahon was a grandson of Hugh O'Neill, Earl of Tyrone. Maguire was born in County Fermanagh and was second Baron of Enniskillen.

The aim of the rising generally was to use surprise rather than military might to achieve their aims in the, perhaps naïve, hope that support from the rest of the country would follow.

The attack on Dublin Castle was foiled when an informer named Owen O'Connolly revealed the plan to the authorities. Mac Mahon and Maguire were arrested and both were later hanged in London.

The first news of the Irish rebellion reached London on 1 November 1641 at a time of the year when the annual commemoration of the failed Gunpowder Plot of 1605 was being prepared. This heightened English sensibilities to the possible effects of the sudden rising. Their fears were confirmed by reports of alleged violent attacks in Ireland on Protestants. Reports to London by Parsons and Borlase were that the 'popish' plot was encouraged 'by the incitement of Jesuits, priests and friars'. At issue in London was what was perceived as a united papist offensive, the origins of which were in Rome, Spain and France and which had as its aim the defeat of Protestantism. It could be said, therefore, that the English response to the 1641 Rising in Ireland reflected an international element rather than a solely domestic one.

Felim O'Neill meanwhile went ahead with the rebellion in the north and enjoyed a measure of success. This was at least partly due to his claiming powers through publishing a royal commission from King Charles to this effect. The commission was a forgery but it did result in his winning some supporters and in enabling him to take several forts in the north of the country. However, O'Neill found that he could not control the Irish peasantry, most of whom had been thrown off their land as a result of the Ulster Plantation and who began attacking Scottish and English Protestants, resulting in severe massacres.

Accounts of the violence were described as creating chaos throughout most of Ulster and along the borders of the Pale. The violence was characterised by widespread instances in which 'the rebels barbarously not only murdered but as we are informed hewed [settlers] to pieces'.

'Settler' refugees made their way to Dublin or to London or other parts of England. Many of the 'depositions', as the reports became known, recorded the losses incurred by Protestant settlers. Thirty-three volumes of depositions were collected and are now housed in the library of Trinity College, Dublin. The grisly descriptions of killings by Catholics of Protestant/English-Scottish settlers may be somewhat exaggerated but even allowing for this it seems sure that many of them can be taken as having some basis in truth.

O'Neill and O'More then tried to march on Dublin but, despite a minor victory at Julianstown near Drogheda in November 1641, the rising started to flounder. This was due to some degree to the delay by the Old English Lords (Catholic) of the Pale to join the active rebellion. These Lords were still bound by ties of blood to the invading power; they were, in feeling, still English. During the period of English settlement in Ireland, their resistance to English power was never the result of any love for the country in which they now settled but was down to private grievances. Their joining belatedly with the Old Irish cause was prompted by the ravaging of Leinster, including the Pale, by the Earl of Ormond, head of the English forces, which left them with little alternative but to support the Old Irish.

The rising did have some success in Munster under the command of Lord Mountgarret and also in Connacht. Although the leaders of the rising were on the side of the monarchy (versus the Parliament) it was in fact the King who joined with Parliament in bargaining successfully, in 1642, with the Scots for an army to suppress Ireland. As a result, in April of that year, General Robert Munro landed with a strong force in Carrickfergus, County Antrim, and was joined by local planters/loyalists. The rising was by now effectively at an end. Later that year, however, the civil war in England (between the Parliamentarians and the Royalists) commenced. This had the effect in Ireland of the two sides becoming more clearly delineated. The Irish Parliament was now wholly Protestant, Catholics being excluded. To counter this, the Catholics formed The Catholic Confederacy of Kilkenny – an assembly of two houses representing the four provinces of the country. The majority of the Confederates were Anglo-Irish Catholics who felt the need to protect their estates, while the native Irish (Old Irish), who had suffered to a far greater degree by confiscation and plantations, were more concerned with recovery of their estates and the preservation of Irish traditions and language. The aims of the Confederation were to procure liberty of conscience, government by Catholics, restitution of lands confiscated by the English, freedom of trade in the Empire and a repealing of Poynings' Law which had denied independence to the Irish Parliament.

AFTERMATH OF THE RISING

Owen Roe O'Neill and General Thomas Preston
In 1642 two famous commanders arrived in Ireland. The first was Owen Roe O'Neill (Eoghan Ruadh Ó Néill), a nephew of the great Hugh O'Neill, Earl of Tyrone. The second was General Thomas Preston, who represented the Old English Catholic side and who had returned from service in the Spanish army. About 200 other Irish officers from Continental armies arrived in Ireland at about this time.

Owen Roe O'Neill was born in Ulster in about 1582. As a result of the 'Flight of the Earls' in 1607, he ended up serving in the Spanish army for about thirty-five years. On his return to Ireland, Owen Roe lost no time in taking command of the Confederate forces in Ulster. Preston, who was put in charge of their forces in Leinster, suffered defeat in a number of battles against Ormond at New Ross in Wexford. From the very start of the Confederation there was a lack of unity. The majority Old English element was anxious to come to terms with the King, while the Old Irish were opposed to this. The separation of Confederate command of forces between the various provinces did not enhance a spirit of unity. A year's truce was arranged by the Earl of Ormond, who held Dublin, but it was not recognised by the Parliamentarians.

Meanwhile a battle of a different nature, namely the struggle in England for power between the King and Parliament, began to move decisively in favour of Parliament. Charles sought help from the Catholic Confederates, but reneged on what was a secret treaty when details of concessions to Catholics leaked out.

Papal Nuncio Rinuccini

In 1645, the Papal Nuncio, Giovanni Battista Rinuccini, landed in Kerry and made for Kilkenny with money from Rome and from the Italian Cardinal Mazarin who had succeeded the influential French Cardinal Richelieu. The provision of this aid was due in no small measure to the endeavours on the Continent of Fr Luke Wadding, head of the Irish Franciscans in Rome. Rinuccini's brief was to restore open Catholicism and to bring Ireland once again under the spiritual authority of the Pope. He recognised in Owen Roe O'Neill someone whose help he needed and could be relied on to win the Catholic cause. His mission being primarily a spiritual one, however, meant that he did not repudiate the monarchy and he possibly thought that his supporters would have been satisfied to have Ireland under a Catholic viceroy of the Crown.

The Battle of Benburb, 1646

A Scottish army had landed in Ulster in 1642, ostensibly to protect the Scottish settlers there from the massacres that followed the rising of 1641. Their aim was to destroy Catholicism and impose Presbyterianism as the 'state' religion. By 1643 they had made significant inroads against the Irish but were prevented from advancing south of mid Ulster, which was held by O'Neill.

In 1646, General Munro, representing the Parliamentarians, assembled an army of about 6,000 men and moved into Owen Roe O'Neill's territory. He had assumed that O'Neill's numerically inferior forces of about 5,000 troops would try to avoid his army and he, therefore, made his soldiers march about 25 kilometres to intercept O'Neill's army at Benburb (south Tyrone). This pre-battle journey was tiring and rendered his men exhausted by the time they reached their destination. On 5 June, O'Neill easily defeated them with relatively few losses on his side.

Instead of capitalising on his victory, O'Neill took his army south to deal with the Confederates whose ratification of a treaty with English Royalists, proposed by Ormond, he strongly opposed. The Papal Nuncio Rinuccini was also opposed to the treaty and went so far as to threaten excommunication of those who supported it. In February 1647 the Confederates relented and rejected it. In that year, too, General Jones commanding the Parliamentarian forces of Dublin completely defeated the Confederates under Preston at Dangan Hill, near Summerhill (west of Maynooth) in County Meath. In addition, the Confederates in the south were routed in Cork by Lord Inchiquin.

Oliver Cromwell

In England the royal cause was almost lost and the army of Oliver Cromwell (which had a major win over the Royalists in the Battle of Naseby in 1645) and the Independents dominated the Long Parliament. Ormond now decided that for him English rebels were better than Irish ones, and he surrendered Dublin to Cromwell's Parliamentary forces.

Oliver Cromwell. Portrait by eighteenth-century English artist John Bulfinch.
© *National Gallery of Ireland.*

Cromwell now had a secure port of entry to Ireland, a fact that was to have a hugely significant impact on Irish history. He arrived in Dublin on 15 April 1649 under the title 'Lord Lieutenant and General for the Parliament of England' with a force of about 20,000 well-equipped troops. Cromwell's intention was to recover Ireland for the Commonwealth or 'Republic' England and to seek revenge for the attacks on Protestant planters for which he wrongly blamed all 'papists'. In September he attacked Drogheda (County Louth) and about 3,000 people, both soldiers and some non-soldiers of both sexes, were brutally put to the sword. He next turned his attention to Wexford, where he adopted the same vicious tactics as he had employed in Drogheda. The brutality of Cromwell's attacks spread terror throughout the country, and the death of Owen Roe O'Neill (thought to have been poisoned by a traitor called Plunkett) in November of 1649 removed from the scene the only commander who might have been able to counter Cromwell with any measure of success. In that same year, Charles I was beheaded by the Parliamentarians, having been found guilty of treason.

In March 1650, the city of Kilkenny surrendered and the Confederation was no more. Cromwell continued his campaign into Munster and in that same year Cromwell suffered his only defeat. It occurred in Clonmel (County Tipperary) when his forces were repulsed by another Hugh O'Neill, a nephew of Owen Roe.

The impact of Cromwell on the Irish landscape was great. He caused significant land confiscations and famously afforded Catholic landowners of Leinster, Munster and Ulster the option of going 'to hell or Connacht', it being the least well-endowed province as regards quality of land and resources. Irish officers surrendered on terms which allowed them to emigrate and find service abroad, while many of those less fortunate were transported in their thousands as slaves to the West Indies.

Fearing a threat from the newly instated King Charles II, Cromwell left Ireland on 26 May 1650 after placing his son-in-law, Ireton, as Lord Lieutenant in charge. There was some subsequent Irish resistance but it all came to an end with the First Siege of Limerick, 1650–1651 (the second occurred in 1690/1691 after the Battle of the Boyne). Disease and starvation forced submission to Ireton of those holding Limerick under Hugh O'Neill.

Galway, too, was under siege by Sir Charles Coote, and with the pressure of famine and disease he forced the surrender of the city in 1652. Protestant control of most aspects of Irish life was now stronger than ever before.

So, the struggle of the Irish, which had commenced with the rising of 1641, was finally over.

LAMENT FOR OWEN ROE O'NEILL

Thomas Davis

– Excerpt –

I

Wail, wail for him through the Island! Weep, weep for our pride!
Would that on the battlefield our gallant chief had died!
Weep the victor of Benburb – weep him young man and old;
Weep for him ye women – your beautiful lies cold!

II

We thought you would not die – we were sure you would not go,
And leave us in our utmost need to Cromwell's cruel blow –
Sheep without a shepherd when the snow shuts out the sky –
Oh! why did you leave us, Owen? Why did you die?

Chapter 4

THE BATTLE OF THE BOYNE

1690

PRINCIPAL CHARACTERS

CHARLES II

JAMES II (JAMES VII OF SCOTLAND)

PRINCE WILLIAM OF ORANGE (WILLIAM III)

RICHARD TALBOT, EARL OF TYRCONNELL
  Commander of James' Troops in Ireland

COUNT FREDERIC SCHOMBERG
  First Leader of William's Forces In Ireland

GENERAL GINKEL
  Second Leader of William's Forces in Ireland

MARSHAL LAUZUN
  General of French Troops on the side of James

GENERAL ST RUTH
  Replacement for Marshal Lauzun

DUKE OF BERWICK
  Son of James II

GENERAL PATRICK SARSFIELD, EARL OF LUCAN
  Leader of Irish Forces under James

BACKGROUND

In 1652, the Cromwellian Act of Settlement was passed by the London Parliament. By this act, 'Irish Papists' were classed according to their 'guilt'. The mass of the poor (those whose possessions were worth not more than £10) were granted a general pardon. Ireland was then effectively divided into two parts: County Clare and the province of Connacht were left to the Irish gentry and landowners and the rest was 'confiscated' to pay arrears of wages to Cromwell's troops. Ireland had, therefore, to pay for its own conquest. Most of the non-landowning class were 'retained', being considered too valuable as labourers to be moved to the west of the country.

On 14 May 1660, in Dublin, Charles II was proclaimed King of Ireland. The restoration of the Stuart monarchy in Ireland was not the work of the Royalist followers but rather that of the Cromwellian leaders. In London, the English Parliament now shared power with the Crown and neither had sympathetic feelings towards the native Irish. Nevertheless, the Irish Catholic leaders considered that only in the monarchy could they have any hope of toleration and of recovery of their lands. Their hopes with regards to religion were based on the 'Declaration of Breda', by which Charles indicated the need for religious toleration. However, additions made to the Penal Laws were soon to remove any such aspirations for the native Irish.

State Church

The Dublin Parliament was a Protestant assembly and public opinion in England did not want any weakening of the 'Protestant and English' interest in Ireland. In this context Charles II himself declared to the Irish: 'My justice I must afford to you all, but my favour must be given to my Protestant subjects.'

Irish Catholics, in arms since the 1641 Rising, were considered to be rebels against the King; it mattered not that they defended their cause solely as Catholic Irish and not by, in any way, repudiating the King. The restoration of the monarchy was matched by that of the State Church (Anglican). This was the only religion that was recognised officially.

In summary, the situation was that a Protestant Anglican ascendancy owned most of the land, notwithstanding the fact that by 1672, of the total population of 1,100,000, Catholics numbered 800,000 (73%) and the Protestants, mainly Presbyterian, only 300,000 (27%).

Trade

Irish trade was greatly restricted by law. An example of this was the enactment of an Irish Cattle Bill, which came about due to the resentment in England by the landlord/farming interests of the importation of cheap cattle from Ireland. Under the ensuing act this importation was forbidden. In addition, various navigation acts also were calculated to adversely affect Irish exports. Under these acts, Irish ships were prevented from exporting to, or importing from, the colonies other than by transportation through England. In effect, Ireland was prevented from normal trading with the Empire for nearly a century.

The Irish Parliament lasted from 1661 to 1666. In 1677, Viceroy Ormond was appointed Lord Lieutenant. It was his intention to convene another Irish Parliament and to extract more subsidies for the Crown by softening the impact of the Act of Settlement (which had imposed penalties, including execution and land confiscation against participants and bystanders of the Irish Rising of 1641) but a 'popish' plot in London, which turned out to be nothing more than a malicious conspiracy, put paid to that. In fact, the Protestant hysteria in England spread to Ireland resulting, for example, in the expelling of the Catholic Archbishop of Armagh, Oliver Plunkett (now Saint Oliver Plunkett) to England where he was tried for an alleged plot to encourage a French invasion of Ireland. He was found guilty of high treason 'for promoting the Roman faith' and was hanged, drawn and quartered at Tyburn on 1 July 1681.

Charles II died on 6 February 1685, and with his demise Ormond ceased to be Lord Lieutenant.

James II

Charles II was succeeded by James II (James VII of Scotland). The fact that he was a Catholic brought some hope to the Catholics of Ireland that their lot, both religious and material, might be improved. This was reinforced by his declared aim to restore Catholicism in England.

The economic situation in Ireland at that time remained poor for the native Irish. This can be illustrated by the fact that their general diet was based on the potato (a situation that repeated itself at the time of the disastrous famine in the 1840s). The local records showed, too, that of the approximately 180,000 houses in Ireland only about 24,000 of them had one chimney or more; the remainder had no such 'luxury'.

Earl of Tyrconnell

James' reign commenced in Ireland by his appointing Colonel Richard Talbot, a Roman Catholic, as viceroy and creating him Earl of Tyrconnell. With the support of the 'Patriot' Parliament held in Dublin in 1689, a parliament that was almost totally Catholic in composition, Talbot set about replacing Protestants with Catholics in the army and in the judiciary. Tyrconnell stood for the old Anglo-Irish party which, however, had little interest in the native race of the Gaelic tradition.

In 1688 a strong feeling against James emerged in England because of his issuing, without referring to Parliament, a 'Declaration of Indulgence' which declared that there was to be complete freedom of religion for all – this despite the fact that Parliament had earlier refused to consent to the proposed law.

William of Orange

In England, the position for Protestants was compounded when a son was born to James. This meant that the English were now faced with a line of Roman Catholic sovereigns. To counter this, an invitation was sent to James' daughter Mary, a confirmed Protestant who was married and living in Holland with her husband, Prince William of Orange, President of the Dutch Republic. The invitation to Mary was that she should become Queen of England, an invitation which she refused unless her husband would be made king. This was agreed. William of Orange landed in England in November 1688, and in 1689 he and Mary began their reign in England.

The resulting dethroning of James in 1688 saw him going to France to seek help from his cousin King Louis XIV to regain his kingdom. The King of France was a fervent Catholic, and also believed, as did James, in the divine right of kings – that is, that kings were chosen by God and that his subjects had no right to rebel against him for any reason whatsoever. More particularly, from Louis' point of view, the fact that he was already at war with William of Orange meant that if William were to become King of England this would make him an even stronger adversary. Louis, therefore, readily supplied James with money, ammunition and French soldiers. With this aid, James returned to Ireland. It was not his intention to remain there, but rather to use it as a base for regaining control of England.

William III (William of Orange). Engraving by eighteenth-century British artist John Smith. © National Gallery of Ireland.

The Siege of Derry, 1688

Northern Ulster, the very centre of Protestantism in Ireland, was the only part of the country to support William of Orange. In December

1688, the citizens of Derry refused to admit a Catholic garrison sent by the Earl of Tyrconnell. The Earl was now the commander of the army in Ireland under James. Protestant supporters from all around Ulster arrived in Derry and took up positions within the strong city walls. The Jacobite (James') army besieged the city for about three months but to no avail. The army was encamped on the land side and a barrier of tree trunks and other objects was stretched across the mouth of the River Foyle, thereby shutting off the only route of relief from the sea. The defenders of the city stood firm despite the usual siege traumas, including starvation, disease and resultant death; indeed, thousands were said to have starved to death. In July 1689, three ships from England bringing food and other supplies broke through the barrier and relieved the city. Realising that all was lost, James' army lifted the siege and departed. Within weeks, Marshal Schomberg landed near Belfast with about 10,000 Williamite troops, and gradually took over the remaining Jacobite strongholds in Ulster.

From his retreat in Dublin, James convened a parliament and had an act passed to allow the restoration to the Irish of the land taken from them during the Cromwellian plantations. Another act was passed to the effect that all Irishmen fighting for William were guilty of high treason. Neither of the acts ever came into force, but they caused much concern in Ulster and in England at the time.

However, the military activity in Ireland was but a part of the great war raging between Louis and his enemies in the League of Augsburg, an alliance which included the Catholic Emperor Leopold and Pope Innocent XI (and later also Pope Alexander VIII). The League objected to French domination in Europe and to Louis' treatment of the Church in France.

THE BATTLE OF THE BOYNE

In the spring of 1690, the French aid for which James had been waiting was finally to hand. Marshal Lauzun arrived in Kinsale from France with 7,000 French troops, including many who were of Dutch or

German nationality. However, James' feelings of relief must have been tempered in June when William of Orange, now under the title of William III of England, landed at Carrickfergus, County Antrim and made for Dublin. William's army was composed of Ulster Protestants, English, Scots, Dutch and Danes. Their numbers included some Catholics, just as on James' side there was a number of Protestants.

James decided to march to face William, despite advice to the contrary from his generals. This he did at the River Boyne near Drogheda, in County Louth.

River Boyne in County Meath.

William's army was the larger of the two, about 36,000 strong as against about 25,000 for James, and was much better equipped with heavy artillery. On the Williamite side, the leaders were William himself and Count Schomberg, an elderly professional soldier who was of German birth but who had been Marshal of France. For James, the generals were Lauzun, Tyrconnell, the Duke of Berwick (James' son) and Patrick Sarsfield.

Portrait of Patrick Sarsfield, Earl of Lucan, by a seventeenth-century English artist.
© *National Gallery of Ireland.*

Sarsfield, a Catholic, was born in Lucan, County Dublin in about 1660. His family was of a Norman origin (by this time 'Old English'). He saw military action in English regiments during the reign of Charles II but returned to Ireland on the accession of James II.

When news reached James that William's forces had crossed the River Boyne, he panicked. He had, in fact, been fooled by perceived decoying actions by William. This resulted in James moving the bulk of his army away from the main battle area, leaving only a small force, without reinforcements, to face the main body of the Williamite army. Failure for the Jacobite forces was, therefore, inevitable and James ordered a retreat. However, he did not wait around to oversee its effects but instead hurried off to Dublin and onwards to Waterford, where he embarked on a ship bound for France.

When the news of the Williamite victory reached London in July it was immediately forwarded to William's allies in the Grand Alliance. Contrariwise, in the Catholic states of Austria and Spain there were celebrations as they were long opposed to Louis' imperial ambitions there. The very nature of the flight of James II was also a cause of celebration to his enemies. To save face, James put the blame for his failure at the Boyne on the Irish troops. Lauzun did likewise, the impact of which was that Irish merchants living in Paris suffered verbal onslaughts from the local populace. James was never to return to Ireland, but remained in France, where he died on 16 September 1701.

After the Boyne debacle, the Irish people realised that James had never had any real sympathy with the national aspirations of the native Irish, but looked on Ireland as nothing more than a convenient route to recover England. Indeed, Tyrconnell had previously declared that it would be better 'for King James to go back to France and leave us to fight our battles in our own way and for our own ends'.

William now took possession of Dublin while what was left of James' forces, both Irish and French, fell back mainly to the west of Ireland. Sarsfield, in charge of the Irish forces, took command of Limerick, while Lauzun and his French troops made for Galway.

The Second Siege of Limerick (Stage 1), 1690
Having been subjected to siege for the first time in 1650, forty years later, Limerick was again faced with siege. On this occasion, it could be said to have occurred in two stages. In the first stage, William laid siege to Limerick, but failed to take the city. This was largely due to the daring exploits of Sarsfield, who managed to intercept and destroy a large quantity of ammunition and artillery that was being sent to

William's camp outside Limerick. The city was thus saved – but only for the moment.

William returned to England and placed General Ginkel, a Dutch soldier, in command in Ireland. In the period 1690/1691, there was not a lot of activity in the country, although Cork and Kinsale were captured in this period by one Viscount Churchill, later Duke of Marlborough.

Athlone

In the Spring of 1691, however, Lauzun returned to France and was replaced by General St Ruth, who arrived with French reinforcements. Almost immediately he was informed that Ginkel was on his way to besiege Athlone (County Westmeath). St Ruth immediately marched to defend Athlone and set up camp on the western side of the town. A bridge joined the two sides of the town, divided by the river Shannon. The western side was considered, strategically, 'the key to Connacht'. Ginkel first captured the 'Leinster' side of the town and then, despite the bridge being destroyed by St Ruth's forces, managed to capture the 'Connacht' side too. St Ruth now withdrew and decided to give further battle instead at Aughrim, near Ballinasloe, in County Galway.

The Battle of Aughrim, 1691

After the fall of Athlone, St Ruth drew up his Jacobite army on a well-chosen and prepared position at Aughrim, County Galway. His lines followed the high ground from the hill of Kilcommedon to Aughrim Castle at the northern end.

In front was an area of bogland. St Ruth's forces withstood several assaults, but in the end, despite their positional advantages, they were defeated, and St Ruth himself was killed in the battle. It was a disastrous loss for the Jacobite side, with about 5,000 killed as against approximately 2,500 on the other side.

Ginkel now moved to Galway, which he took at the end of July, and then proceeded to Limerick, which he now subjected to a further siege.

Memorial cross on the site of the Battle of Aughrim (County Galway) at the place where the Jacobite leader General St Ruth was killed.

The Second Siege of Limerick (Stage 2), 1691, and the Treaty of Limerick
Sarsfield was once again the leader of the defending forces. Ginkel attacked the city with some success and, although the Jacobite army defended as well as it could, it soon became clear to Sarsfield that they could not hold out much longer. Therefore, in September, after a period of one month, the Irish and French generals concluded that further resistance was useless. Negotiations were opened in which Sarsfield played a prominent part and by early October a draft treaty was signed.

Under the terms of the Treaty of Limerick, the Irish Roman Catholics were to have the same religious freedom as granted during the reign of Charles II. Secondly, Catholics were to be allowed to hold public positions subject to their taking an oath of allegiance (the Oath of Supremacy was not to apply to them). Additionally, none of the Jacobite officers or soldiers was to be deprived of their land and, finally, all officers and soldiers were to be allowed either to go abroad or join the Williamite army.

Treaty Stone. Near Thomond Bridge, Limerick.

The Wild Geese

Led by Sarsfield, something between 12,000 to 20,000 soldiers chose to leave Ireland and take up service in France, Spain and Austria. These became known as the 'Wild Geese', and many of them rose to high levels in the armies and governments of the countries to which they flew.

Sarsfield was to die fighting for France in the battle of Neerwinden in Holland on 19 August 1693. As he lay dying he was reported to have said 'if only it was for Ireland'. He is buried in the grounds of

St Martin Church in Huy, Belgium where a plaque on the wall of the church marks the spot.

Those who remained in Ireland, however, soon found that the terms of the Treaty of Limerick were in effect largely ignored by the English side. The result of this was that the Irish Catholics had to endure even harsher times than those previously prevailing. Also, Jacobite estates were forfeited to the Crown or sold off to friends of King William.

Penal Laws

The Irish now suffered under the Penal Laws, which were first implemented during the reign of William III. (The Penal Laws were passed at different periods: William III (1688–1702), Anne (1702–1714), and George I (1714–1727).)

The areas of Irish life that the Penal Laws affected can be divided into four categories: religion, land, public life and education.

Religion

Under the Penal Laws, all Roman Catholic bishops, priests (especially Jesuits), monks and nuns were ordered to leave the country. Those who did not do so, or who returned, were transported to the West Indies as slaves. Some parish priests were allowed to stay in Ireland, but it was necessary for them to register and give an undertaking of 'good behaviour' and take an oath of allegiance.

Land

No Roman Catholic, apart from a few who, due to the influence of William, had been allowed to retain their estates after the Treaty of Limerick, was allowed to own land. Roman Catholics were not permitted to take land on a lease for a period longer than thirty-nine years. The few Roman Catholic landowners favoured by William could not bequeath their estate to the eldest son but must divide it among all of them. However, if the eldest son became a Protestant, the whole estate would vest in him exclusively.

Public Life

No Roman Catholic could vote at either parliamentary or municipal elections, nor could he be a Member of Parliament, a judge, juryman, coroner or lawyer. No Roman Catholic could enter the army or royal navy or civil service. He could not be a printer, a cutler or a gunmaker. No Protestant manufacturer could take on a Roman Catholic apprentice. This meant, consequently, that the great majority of Roman Catholics in the eighteenth century were either shopkeepers or workers of the land.

Education

No Roman Catholic could enter a university or keep a school, nor was he allowed to have a Roman Catholic tutor to teach his children at home or to send his children abroad to be educated.

Continuing Repression

The Penal Laws were so numerous and applied to so many people in Ireland that it was, in practice, not possible to implement them in many cases. It was difficult for the authorities, even by the lure of large rewards, to track down all of the unregistered priests who lived in concealment and who held religious services on hilltops and in remote districts. Presbyterians, being dissenters, suffered in the same way as Catholics. The Penal Laws were not repealed until the end of the eighteenth century, although in practice they were ignored from about 1770 onwards. They were, however, the cause of large-scale emigration. In general Catholics went to France, Spain and Austria while the Presbyterians went to North America. Those who remained behind in Ireland were demoralised by being deprived of any hope of improving their subservient lot. They clung to their religion despite having to suffer significantly for it.

The conditions under which tenants held their land were grossly punitive. Rents, already appallingly high, were uncontrolled, which meant that any improvements a farmer made to his home or land resulted in an increase in rent. Many, therefore, avoided making any such improvements for fear of being charged more rent. This resulted in many of them living in squalor. Tenants also had to pay tithes to the local Anglican Church, irrespective of what religion they espoused. Tenants had no fixity of tenure, which meant that even if they paid their rent they could be turned out at the whim of the landlord.

The Anglicans, on the other hand, were a small, favoured class surrounded by those who greatly resented them; even long after the Penal Laws had been repealed, the feeling of resentment of the Irish against them was to last.

Poetry

A perhaps unusual fact of history during the Penal days was the impact of poetry on the native Irish population. In the midst of severe persecution, poets in every province of Ireland 'sang' to the people in their own language. This poetry possessed an aspect distinct from a purely literary one; namely, it displayed the social life of the times and the outlook and attitude of the people, which was very different to that portrayed by the writers of English or that voiced in the Irish Parliament. The frequent references to characters of Greek mythology and Latin literature demonstrate that the traditions of old scholarship had been retained to a significant extent in the 'hedge-schools'. These 'peasant' poets were in particular abundance in Munster, although every county produced poets of some recognised merit. Particular examples were Eoghan Ó Ráthaille and Eoghan Ó Súilliabháin (Kerry) and Seoghan 'Clárach' Mac Domhnaill (Cork).

Conclusion

The hopes of the native Irish people, always overshadowed by those of the 'upper classes', which might possibly have been realised at least to some extent with the reign of James II, were now dashed. Clearly, they would have no choice but to await another day for better times to come.

Chapter 5

THE 1798 RISING

PRINCIPAL CHARACTERS

THEOBALD WOLFE TONE
  Main Leader of the Rising

LORD EDWARD FITZGERALD
  Leader of the Rising

GENERAL HOCHE
  General of the French Army destined for Ireland, 1796

GENERAL HUMBERT
  General of the French Army in Ireland, 1798

HENRY GRATTAN
  Member of the Irish Parliament

HENRY FLOOD
  Member of the Irish Parliament

WILLIAM PITT
  British Prime Minister

FR JOHN MURPHY
  Leader of the Rising in Wexford

GENERAL LAKE
  Commander of the British Forces in Ireland

BACKGROUND

Hanoverian rule commenced in England and, consequently, in Ireland with the accession to the throne of George I in 1714. It provided no relief in the matter of freedom of religious expression in Ireland and Catholicism was to remain driven underground. Nevertheless, the native Irish clung tenaciously to their religion and also to their own language.

In the period 1714–1760, relative calm prevailed on the political front. Ireland continued to be ruled from Westminster and this was done in the interests of England in its relationship with a subject kingdom. Ireland remained totally disarmed, leaving an English army of 12,000 men in Ireland untroubled.

The Irish Parliament, totally controlled in the interests of England, met only once every second year or so. The life of the Parliament was virtually unlimited and one convened by George II lasted thirty-three years (from 1727 to 1760). In any event, under Poynings' Law (a law introduced by Sir Edward Poynings in the Irish Parliament in 1495), it was not possible for an Irish parliament to pass any act unacceptable to the English government. Meanwhile, the upper classes in Ireland displayed submission and loyalty to England, while the ordinary Irish natives would probably have engaged in a popular rising were they to receive French support once again.

Indeed, at about this time, a widespread agrarian movement was being formed. This was especially so in Munster and was aimed against high rents, continuing lack of tenure, tithes and other taxes. The old Irish nation with its Gaelic traditions remained suppressed but was not dead.

After years of pursuing a degree of independence for the Irish Parliament, led initially by Henry Flood and later by Henry Grattan, it was finally granted in 1782.

The seat of 'Grattan's Parliament' (now the property of The Bank of Ireland).

Henry Grattan was born in Dublin on 3 July 1746. He received his early education at Mr Ball's school in Great Ship Street, Dublin (to the rear of Dublin Castle). Later he attended Mr Young's school in Abbey Street before entering Trinity College, Dublin. He was called to the Bar in 1772. He moved from law to politics and was elected to the Irish Parliament in 1775.

Statue of Henry Grattan at College Green, Dublin. Sculptor: John Henry Foley.

The parliament in Dublin became known as 'Grattan's Parliament'. For about the next eighteen years, the rights of Ireland as a sister kingdom to its English counterpart were in place. The primary aim of the members of the Irish Parliament was to confirm their position as the dominant minority within Irish society. In confirmation of this, Henry Flood said in 1783:

> Ninety years ago four fifths of Ireland were for King James. They were defeated. I rejoice in that defeat. The laws that followed were not laws of persecution; they were a political necessity. What will be the consequence if you give Catholics equal powers with Protestants? We will give all toleration to religion. We will not give them political power.

The Relaxing of the Penal Laws

By the abolition of the greater part of the penal code in 1782, the upper and middle classes of Roman Catholics were permitted to acquire property and enjoy some elements of the status of citizenship. However, although Grattan was in favour of the granting of full emancipation and to admitting Catholics to the franchise, to Parliament, and to all but the highest offices, he did not receive support in this from his fellow 'Patriot' leaders. 'Grattan's Parliament' did, however, deliver a period of significant prosperity to Ireland.

The Corn Law

An Irish Corn Law was introduced in 1784, under which Ireland became a great corn growing country, well able to satisfy the home market as well as selling its surplus to England. Under this law, too, it was prohibited to import foreign grain unless in circumstances of acute scarcity. Ireland now became for the first time ever a great tillage country. This resulted in increased revenue for the Dublin Parliament, which, in turn, endowed public utilities (e.g. canal building) and the refurbishment of public buildings in Dublin city. Landlords benefited from this new export trade which was made to satisfy increasing needs arising from the Industrial Revolution in Britain. Great corn mills flourished as a result of the general uplifting of trade and the ensuing prosperity led to building of fine country mansions and houses. All of this was of little benefit to the native Irish population and may, indeed, have fuelled the seeds of the rebellion that was to come later.

Discontent

Discontent among the native Irish regarding their lot continued, a major cause of which was the hated tithe system. Much further afield, however, there was also discontent at this time among the populace of North America and of France. The movement in France turned decidedly in the direction of revolution, while news from America of an emerging 'free country' added to the growth of republican sentiments among the Irish population.

Reform of Parliament

Both Grattan and Flood were intent on reforming the Irish Parliament, the hallmarks of which were cronyism and blatant corruption. However, as long as a majority in Parliament could be 'bought' to support British policy it was unlikely that Parliament would be reformed. Additionally, the wealthier Ireland became and the more equality she attained with England, the more England considered it necessary to continue to control her; so, any reformation of Parliament was bound to fail. In these circumstances it was not surprising that the matter of Catholic emancipation was suspended.

In 1785, there was a proposal, accepted by the Irish Parliament, by which there would be free trade between Ireland and England in return for Ireland contributing some surplus revenue to support the imperial navy. Commercial jealousy in England, however, resulted in the proposal being considerably constrained by Prime Minister Pitt.

LEAD-UP TO THE RISING

Theobald Wolfe Tone

Wolfe Tone was born of Protestant yeoman stock at Stafford Street, Dublin on 20 June 1763. The street is now named after him. He was baptised in the nearby parish church of St Mary's.

Statue of Wolfe Tone by sculptor Edward Delaney, St Stephen's Green, Dublin 2.

The Tones were descended from a French Protestant family which fled to England from France in the sixteenth century to escape religious persecution. A branch of the family moved to Dublin sometime in the seventeenth century. Wolfe Tone's father, Peter Tone, sold his farm and became a coach-maker in Dublin. His mother, whose family name was Lambert, was a Catholic who converted to Protestantism shortly after Wolfe Tone was born.

St Mary's Church, Mary Street, Dublin 2, and its baptismal font at which Wolfe Tone was baptised. Courtesy of The Church café, bar, restaurant, Mary Street, Dublin.

Tone received his early education with two of his brothers at an 'English' school in Dublin kept by Sisson Darling. After three years, he attended another school in Henry Street, Dublin, run by Reverend William Craig. In 1781 he entered Trinity College, Dublin where he studied law. He married Martha (Matilda) Witherington of Grafton Street, Dublin in the nearby St Anne's Church in Dawson Street.

> I was then a scholar of the house in the university, and every day, I used to walk under her window with one or other of my fellow students. I soon grew passionately fond of her, and she also, was struck with me, though certainly my appearance, neither then nor now, was much in my favour; so it was, however, that, before we had ever spoken to each other, a mutual affection had commenced between us.

Tone was called to the Bar in 1789. His thoughts slowly turned from the practice of law to those of politics and he soon came to the conclusion that: 'Ireland would neither be free, prosperous or happy, until she was independent and that independence was unattainable whilst the connection with England existed.'

Tone found that the Irish Parliament was ineffective, being only an assembly of landlords or their nominees and government placements. Only sixty-four of the 300 Members of Parliament were elected. The nobility and landed gentry nominated about 200 members and the rest, whose role was to do what Dublin Castle (the seat of British control) told them to do, were placed by the government. In effect, the British cabinet decided the fate of Irish bills.

Trouble in France

On 21 January 1793 Louis XVI was executed by guillotine and the French Republic, already at war with Austria and Prussia, declared war on England. What were seen as the horrors and revolutionary principles at play in France created panic in the conservative ruling classes in both Britain and Ireland.

The British Parliament under Pitt, supported by Irishman Edmund Burke, considered that it was an inopportune time for implementing reforms in Ireland. The Roman Catholic Church in Ireland was opposed to the French Revolution, but the radical teaching of the newly emerged United Irishmen appealed to the native Irish Catholics and Presbyterians, who were living in a situation where the members of the Protestant Church of Ireland possessed all of the jobs and owned five sixths of the land while forming only one tenth of the population. Meanwhile, Grattan was fully supportive of the Irish Parliament's pledge to support England in the war against France. Any further attempts at reform of Parliament were thwarted by the English Parliament on the basis that England was busily engaged in the struggle against France.

The United Irishmen

On 18 October 1791, a political club in Belfast, the membership of which included Thomas Russell, Robert and William Simms and others such as Henry Joy Mc Cracken, formed a radical reform movement called the Society of United Irishmen. Tone was invited to join and draw up its draft constitution. The primary aims of this new movement were, firstly, to create the union of all the people of Ireland to counterbalance the weight of English influence in an effort to preserve the liberty of the people and their commerce and, secondly, a complete and radical reform of the representation of the people in Parliament. Additionally, the movement considered that reform could not be just, practical or efficacious if it did not include Irishmen of every religious persuasion. Tone pointed out that:

> We have no national government. We are ruled by Englishmen and the servants of Englishmen, filled as to commerce and politics, with the short-sighted and ignorant prejudice of their country; and these men have the whole power and patronage of Ireland as means to seduce and subdue the honesty and spirit of her representatives in the legislature.

The Dublin Society of the United Irishmen was formed in November 1791 with James Napper Tandy as its secretary. Dr Thomas Addis Emmet (a brother of Robert Emmet), who was a close friend of Tone, was also a member, as were Henry Joy Mc Cracken and Oliver Bond.

Wolfe Tone set out his political and social democratic views in a number of pamphlets. His publication 'An Argument on Behalf of the Catholics of Ireland' was particularly significant. It was an address to the Protestants of Ulster with the aim of bringing both Catholics and Protestants together in order to break the connection with England. As a result of the publication of this pamphlet, Tone was invited by the leaders of the Catholic Committee to become their secretary. This was a notable move in that, up to that time, Tone was said not to have known a single Catholic; now, almost overnight, he had become a leading figure in their cause.

James Napper Tandy. English nineteenth-century engraving.
© National Gallery of Ireland.

The Catholic Committee had been formed in 1756, but their ambitions up to now were limited, seeking only to recover some civil rights whilst remaining subservient to a Protestant constitution.

Tone stated:

What answer could we make to the Catholics of Ireland, if they were to rise, and with one voice, demand their rights as citizens, and as men? What reply, justifiable to God, and to our conscience? None. We prate and babble, and write books and publish them, filled with sentiments of freedom, and abhorrence of tyranny, and of lofty praises of the Rights of Man! Yet we are content to hold three million of our fellow creatures, and fellow subjects, in degradation and in infamy, and contempt, or to sum up all in one word, in Slavery!

Tone became heavily engaged in organising the setting up of a Catholic convention. It assembled in December 1792 in Tailors' Hall in Dublin.

Approximately 280 delegates attended. Its aim was to push for the abolition of all remaining Penal Laws still in effect in Ireland. Dublin Castle made a number of indirect attempts to stop the convention, but ultimately failed.

Tailors' Hall, Back Lane, Dublin 8, near Christ Church Cathedral. Tailors' Hall is the oldest surviving Guild Hall in Dublin, restored and now the home of An Taisce – The National Trust for Ireland.

In the previous year, John Keogh, a Dublin tradesman, had come to the fore as the leader of the Catholic Committee. The Committee pushed for Catholic emancipation and, although both Pitt and Grattan favoured movement in this direction, the Catholic Relief Bill of

1792 granted only minor concessions. Due to the intervention of King George IV, however, the corresponding act (of 1793) was passed by the House of Commons in London. It allowed Catholics to bear arms, to become members of corporations, to vote in borough elections in the counties (albeit only as forty-shilling freeholders), to take degrees in Trinity College, Dublin and to take minor offices. They were, though, effectively debarred from taking seats in Parliament by the need to take an oath of allegiance which was repugnant to them.

Protestants and Catholics

Meanwhile, the long-standing feuds between Protestants and Catholics in Ulster resulted in an armed encounter in Armagh which, in turn, resulted, on 21 September in 1795, in the establishment of the Orange Order. The aims of the Order were 'to maintain the laws and peace of the country and the Protestant Constitution and to defend the King and his heirs as long as they shall maintain the Protestant ascendancy'.

The Orange Order soon numbered thousands of militant Protestants. The continuing conflict resulted in many Catholics being driven into Connacht, while the more adventurous of them opted to join the United Irishmen. In 1796, an Insurrection Act was passed which allowed the Lord Lieutenant of Ireland to introduce martial law. The death penalty was now to apply for administering an 'unlawful' oath and transportation for life for the taking of such an oath.

From an English perspective, Ulster was becoming a dangerous province. The Irish had accumulated arms and the Presbyterians were mainly sworn United Irishmen. Lord Camden, who was Lord Lieutenant at this time, ordered the disarming of Ulster and this was carried out in 1797 with ruthless brutality. In a move to counter the strength of Ulster 'rebels', the English government set up a yeomanry armed force comprised of Protestant tenants and townspeople commanded by local gentry.

The actions of the English regular troops, together with about 50,000 yeomanry, to suppress any acts of rebellion resulted in the view of many Irish people being that 'union with France' would be preferable to 'union with Britain'. By this time, Ireland's population was about four and a half million, of whom three quarters were native Irish peasants. 150,000 Irish were thought to be members of the United Irishmen.

Realising that the Irish Parliament was never going to be a realistic vehicle in obtaining political freedom, Tone drew up plans to seek military assistance from France for a rising in Ireland. The plans were discovered by the British and Tone was forced to flee to the United States of America. While there, Tone petitioned the French Minister to the USA for permission to travel to France. He sailed for France on 1 January 1796, where he convinced the French government, already at war with Britain, to provide military assistance to Ireland.

Lord Edward Fitzgerald

One of the leaders of the United Irishmen was Lord Edward Fitzgerald, the fifth son of the Duke of Leinster. He was born in Carton House, County Kildare on 15 October 1763. His family moved to France when he was about ten years old. His education was conducted by William Ogilvie, his mother's second husband (her first husband had died at a young age). Lord Edward was trained for a military career from an early age and this continued with his full and enthusiastic cooperation when, later, the family moved to England. Not long after his admission to the British army he was sent with a troop to relieve what was, from a British perspective, 'a bad situation', namely, the American War of Independence. His destination was Charleston. He also saw action in South Carolina and was wounded badly in the thigh. He was found by a poor American slave, who carried him on his back to his hut where he nursed him back to health. In gratitude, Lord Edward took the man, nicknamed 'Faithful Tony', into his service for the rest of his life.

After service in America, Lord Edward served in the West Indies (St Lucia) and Canada and thereafter in England before moving back to Ireland. He became a supporter of Grattan but later realised that the Irish Parliament was limited to narrow ascendancy interests. He then developed instead a strong interest in the nationalist cause.

Lord Edward was an inveterate letter writer and kept in constant contact with his mother when he was away from home. His regard for her was very evident from the content and style of his writing. This can be illustrated by the following excerpt from a letter from Lord Edward to his mother while he was away in Paris:

It is time for me to go to Frascati [home in Blackrock, County Dublin]. Why are you not there, dearest of mothers? But it will feel a little like seeing you to go there. We shall talk a great deal of you. I assure you I miss you in Ireland very, very much. I am not half so merry as I should be if you were here ... you are, after all, what I love best in the world.

Carton House, incorporating Carton House Hotel.

It was in the course of a visit to Paris in 1792 that his admiration grew for the aims of the French Revolution of 1789, and he began to see how similar aspirations might apply in Ireland. It was also during this visit to Paris that he met, and one year later married, Mademoiselle Pamela Sims. She was the daughter of a Madame de Genlis but it was not clear who exactly her father was. They were, in any event, very much in love and Pamela gave birth to two children.

In 1796, Lord Edward joined the United Irishmen.

Portrait of Lord Edward Fitzgerald, by Hamilton. Courtesy of the Mallaghan family of Carton House.

Tone in Paris

When Wolfe Tone arrived in Paris from America, he so impressed the French that he was given the rank of Adjutant General in the French army. Meanwhile, members of the United Irishmen who had travelled to Hamburg received Lord Edward Fitzgerald, who had also travelled there. Fitzgerald's role was to meet the French Minister to Hanseatic towns and to encourage the French, who were in control there, to send aid to Ireland. The French Foreign Minister said that if aid were to be given the French would not remain in Ireland any longer than was necessary to expel the English. The Minister's principal aim, therefore, was to be able to demonstrate their superior military strength to the English. While Fitzgerald thought that the receipt of arms from France would, in itself, be sufficient for their needs, Tone, being the more realistic of the two, knew that a French army of about 20,000 soldiers would be needed for any chance of success. In this regard the Dublin-born Duke of Wellington later commented:

> Wolfe Tone was a most extraordinary man. With one hundred guineas in his pocket, unknown and un-recommended he went to Paris in order to overthrow the British Government in Ireland. He asked for a large force. Lord Edward Fitzgerald for a small one. They listened to Tone.

First Attempted Aid from France

After much persuading on the part of Tone and many delays, some of which were due to bad weather, the French agreed to send an army to Ireland. On 15 December 1796, a fleet of forty-three ships under the command of General Hoche set sail from Brest. Tone was in one of them. Part of the fleet arrived in Bantry Bay on 22 December, but a strong easterly gale blew for a week and made it impossible for them to put ashore.

An excerpt from Tone's diary of 25 December 1796 illustrates the position:

> Last night I had the strongest expectations that today we should debark, but at two this morning I was awakened by the wind. I rose immediately and wrapping myself in my great coat, walked for an hour in the gallery, devoured by the most gloomy reflections. The wind continues right ahead, so that it is absolutely impossible to work up to the landing-place, and God knows when it will change. The same wind is exactly favourable

to bring the English upon us, and these cruel delays give the enemy time to assemble his entire force in this neighbourhood, and perhaps (it is, unfortunately, more than perhaps) by his superiority in numbers, in cavalry, in artillery, in money, in provisions, in short in everything we want, to crush us, supposing we are even able to effectuate a landing at last, at the same time that the fleet will be caught as in a trap. Had we been able to land the first day and march directly to Cork, we should have infallibly carried it by a coup de main, and then we should have a footing in the country; but as it is, if we are taken, my fate will not be a mild one; the best I can expect is to be shot as an émigré renter, unless I have the good fortune to be killed in the action; for, most assuredly, if the enemy will have us, he must fight for us. Perhaps I may be reserved for a trial, for the sake of striking terror into others, in which case I shall be hanged as a traitor, and embowelled etc. As to the embowelling, je m'en fiche: if ever they hang me, they are welcome to embowel me if they please. These are pleasant prospects! Nothing on earth could sustain me now, but the consciousness that I am engaged in a just and righteous cause. For my family, I have, by a desperate effort, surmounted my natural feelings so far that I do not think of them at this moment. This day, at twelve, the wind blows a gale still from the east, and our situation is now as critical as possible, for it is mortally certain that this day or tomorrow in the morning, the English fleet will be in the harbour's mouth, and then adieu to everything ... My prospects at this hour are as gloomy as possible. I see nothing before, unless a miracle be wrought in our favour, but the ruin of the expedition, the slavery of my country, and my own destruction. Well, if I am to fall, at least I will sell my life as dear as individual resistance can make it. So now I have made up my mind. I have a merry Christmas of it to-day.

In the end, the expedition had to return to France with Hoche himself, along with the remainder of the fleet, never landing on Irish soil.

The Irish Parliament made a final appeal to the British government in March 1797 to placate the country by accepting a reform of Parliament and a measure of religious freedom. Neither the King nor his English Parliament, however, was in favour of this and so the day of an inevitable rising in Ireland grew ever nearer.

Second Attempted Aid from France

In June 1797 a second attempt on the part of France to help Ireland was planned. This entailed the sending of a French-Dutch fleet with 14,000 men. The fleet set sail in October but was met and defeated in a major naval action in the North Sea, off Camperdown, Holland. The Royal fleet was under the command of Admiral Adam Duncan, while the French-Dutch opposition was commanded by Vice Admiral Jan de Winter. Hoche, who participated, did not survive and this left Napoleon Bonaparte as the best of the remaining French generals. Bonaparte considered that there was little chance of success in Ireland and that any help from France now could only be insignificant. In his biography of Lord Edward Fitzgerald, Thomas Moore referred in the following terms to Bonaparte's slowness to grant aid to Ireland:

> It is not to be wondered at, therefore, that a race like the Irish, among whom rebellion had, he knew, been handed down, from age to age, as a sort of birth-right should be regarded by the candidate for empire with no very friendly eye.

With the imminent demise of the last parliament of the 'Kingdom of Ireland' (before its union with that of Britain), the military command of the English in Ireland fell to General Lake.

THE 1798 RISING

In the knowledge that French aid would not arrive, the United Irishmen decided on a rising without it. A general insurrection was planned for 23 May 1798.

The strength of rebel forces was specified in a document, presented by Lord Edward to the leaders of the United Irishmen, as follows:

	Armed Men	Finances in Hand
ULSTER	110,990	£436-2-4
MUNSTER	100,634	£147-17-2
KILDARE	10,863	£110-17-7
WICKLOW	12,895	£ 93-6-4
DUBLIN	3,010	£37-2-6
DUBLIN CITY	2,177	£321-17-11
QUEEN'S COUNTY *(Laois)*	11,689	£91-2-1
KING'S COUNTY *(Offaly)*	3,600	£21-11-3
CARLOW	9,414	£49-2-10
KILKENNY	624	£10-2-3
MEATH	1,400	£171-2-1
Total	267,296	£1,490-4-4

Unfortunately, the person to whom this information was first disclosed was one Thomas Reynolds, an informer.

As regards the number of rebels, subsequent conversations by Lord Edward indicated that in the event of a call to action the actual number of men would likely to be about 100,000.

The government, having been appraised of the proposed rising, moved early to arrest a number of the main leaders. Indeed, there were many informers who kept the British government well advised on the activities of the rebels. The Shears brothers, Harry and John, were among the first rebels to be apprehended and they were sent to the gallows.

Lord Edward initially escaped the clutches of the English soldiers and for a few weeks roamed around County Dublin in disguise. On one occasion, while dressed as a woman, two 'minders' accompanying him became alarmed when they heard voices behind them of people they assumed were in pursuit, and they urged Lord Edward to lay himself down in a ditch by the roadside until the people had passed by. When they had done so Lord Edward emerged from the ditch covered up to his chin in mud and 'was to himself a source of jest and amusement'.

Later, he rode out with a companion to reconnoitre the line of the proposed advance on the Kildare side to Dublin. He was stopped by a patrol at Palmerston, but was well disguised. He represented himself to be a doctor on his way to a dying patient and was allowed to go on his way.

Sometime later again, however, just before the rising, Lord Edward was betrayed and was badly wounded in the course of being arrested. In the scuffle one of his attackers, a man by the name of Ryan, suffered a severe wound from which he later died. Lord Edward himself died some days later, on 4 June 1798. He was just thirty-four years old. He was laid to rest in the vaults of St Werburgh's Church (Church of Ireland) in Dublin's Werburgh Street.

On his deathbed, a military man who had known him from his time in Charleston alluded to the circumstances under which they had first met. Lord Edward's comment was: 'Ah, I was wounded there in a very different cause – that was fighting *against* liberty – this is fighting *for* it.'

Wolfe Tone, meanwhile, was still in France. But in Ireland there was little activity by the rebels in Munster or Connacht, although poorly armed men rose in Leinster (Wexford, Wicklow, Kildare, Carlow and Meath) only to be quickly suppressed or simply massacred by mounted troops.

Wexford and Wicklow

The most concentrated aspect of the rising took place in Wexford. The county had been a stronghold of Normans and Saxons since their invasion of the area in 1169, and the southern parts were now inhabited by Old English whose language was an old Saxon dialect. The northern parts, though, were Irish and it was here that the United Irishmen rose. The government troops acted quickly and with a brutality which they had already displayed in other parts of the country. Their approach was aggravated by the fact that they were largely Orange yeomen who considered that they were conducting a religious war.

Statue of a Pikeman in Wexford town.

On 26 May, action commenced in Wexford, led by Fr John Murphy of Boolavogue. Although poorly armed with only pikes, they enjoyed a number of successes, which had the effect of increasing the number of volunteers to their cause. They soon occupied the town of Wexford and went on to control most of the county. In order to capitalise on their position, they needed to break through to the surrounding counties. On 1 June, they lost at Newtownbarry when trying to get into Wicklow. Despite this, they did have success two days later at Gorey when they managed to open up a route to Dublin along the coast, but for some reason they then failed to make use of it.

At New Ross, on 4 June, action by about 15,000 pikemen began under the command of a Protestant leader, Bagenal Harvey. Despite the meagreness of their arms, they eventually overcame the opposition of General Jackson (in the Battle of Ross), whose troops numbered only about 1,400. Their success was short-lived as Jackson, seeing that many of the rebels were concentrating on celebrating their success with alcohol, rallied and drove them out of the town leaving some 2,000 of them dead.

The town of Arklow now became a focal point for action when, on 9 June 1798, another group of rebels – led this time by another Catholic priest, Father Michael Murphy – made a determined attack there. They numbered about 19,000 ill-armed men. They had good success until the death of their leader disheartened them, and they succumbed to superior armoury and to the well-fortified position of the British troops.

Brutality

It is not unusual in battles that atrocities are committed on both sides. It may be that some accounts are exaggerated for purposes of propaganda. The accuracy of the descriptions of these atrocities may, therefore, be open to question.

Myles Byrne, who took part in the rising, stated:

The State of the country prior to the Insurrection is not to be imagined except by those who witnessed the atrocities of every description committed by the military and the Orangemen who were let loose on the unfortunate defenceless and unarmed population.

And again:

Though the priests were not at first in favour of any rising, yet, as we know, on account of the atrocities committed on the people, Father John Murphy, of Boolavogue, advised that 'they had better die courageously in the field than be butchered in their houses'.

In responding to the 1798 Rising, the British army resorted to the standard punishment of the day, which was flogging. Wooden triangles were erected for this purpose and punishment could be anything from 500 to 1,000 lashes. Needless to say, many did not survive this punishment. Pitch capping was also administered, in which brown paper caps were filled with hot pitch and placed on a prisoner's head and, when cooled, set on fire. The cap could not be removed without taking with it lumps of skin. Half-hanging and full hanging were also resorted to.

There are also corresponding accounts of brutality administered by the rebels against the enemy. In a book published in 1829 by George Taylor entitled *History of the Rise, Progress and Suppression of the Rebellion in County Wexford – 1798* the following accounts are given:

White Boys, wearing white shirts which were thrown over their clothes, seized all the horses they could find, then set off at full speed in great bodies to the destined place and proceeded to dig up the pastures, burn houses, barns and stacks of corn, drag out the proctors [agents for the collection of tithes], cut off their noses and ears, horse whip them nearly to death and sometimes bury them alive; and all this to prevent their gathering the tithes.

And again, in relation to an attack on Protestants in Scullabogue:

One part massacred those in the dwelling house, the other, all that were confined in the barn. Thirty-seven were taken from the dwelling house and shot. The barn was set on fire – the doors held closed – eventually Protestants broke through but were 'piked'... There was a woman in the barn who, finding no way to escape the flames, she thought if possible, to save her child. She accordingly wrapped her cloak about the infant and threw it out of the barn, but one of the sanguinary pikemen thrust his weapon through the helpless babe and giving a great shout cried: "D—n you, you little heretic, get in there" and instantly flung it into the fire.

Vinegar Hill

Thousands of English militia now arrived in Ireland while the 'Wexford' rebels made their headquarters at Vinegar Hill at Enniscorthy.

On 21 June, General Lake with an army of about 13,000 soldiers stormed the rebels, bringing the uprising there to an end after a battle which saw hundreds of rebels, including women and children, killed. Many, however, managed to escape. There was one last effort made by a small contingent of men under Fr John Murphy. They made their way into County Kilkenny but were defeated and Fr Murphy was captured and executed. A few minor incidents continued and a number of the rebels made their way into the Wicklow hills where, under Joseph Holt and Michael Dwyer, guerrilla warfare continued for a time.

Battle of Vinegar Hill, Enniscorthy, County Wexford.

Plaque at the Croppies' Acre, Wolfe Tone Quay, Dublin.

Actions in Ulster

There were two principal leaders engaged in the rising in Ulster. These were Henry Joy Mc Cracken and Henry Munro.

Mc Cracken was born in Belfast on 31 August 1767. His father, Captain John Mc Cracken, a Presbyterian, was a ship owner and rope-maker. His mother, whose maiden name was Joy, was of Huguenot descent and was also a Presbyterian. In 1796, Mc Cracken was imprisoned for a year in Kilmainham Gaol in Dublin for activities associated with his membership of the United Irishmen (of which he was a founder). In the rising he led his forces of several thousand men in an attack on Antrim town. They were repulsed, and shortly afterwards Mc Cracken was captured. He was tried for treason and hanged in Belfast's Cornmarket on 17 June 1798.

Henry Munro was born in Lisburn in 1758. His father was a Presbyterian but died when Henry was very young and Henry's mother raised her son in the Anglican tradition. Munro became an ardent advocate of Catholic rights. He joined the United Irishmen in 1795. At the outbreak of the rising he and his forces occupied Ballynahinch in Down. There they were attacked by superior forces led by General Nugent. Munro's men were overpowered, pikemen being no match for artillery, and Munro was captured. He was executed at Lisburn on 16 June 1798.

The Battle of Tara

Following the failure of the rebellion in Dublin, Wexford and Wicklow, many rebels made their way to County Meath with the aim of setting up a camp on the Hill of Tara. The location was picked as it provided strategic control of road access to Dublin. Nevertheless, given their lack of arms, it would seem an unsuitable site for the rebels to select for battle against much superior forces. Approximately 5,000 men assembled there on 26 May 1798. Cavalry action and cannon fire by the English forces soon brought the battle to a bloody close. It was estimated that between 400 and 500 rebels were killed against English losses of about thirty soldiers.

Mass grave of those who died in 1798 at Hill of Tara, marked by the ancient Lia Fáil standing stone which had been moved from a nearby location.

The French Again – Third Attempt

On 17 June, the Irish Parliament passed an act of amnesty which led to the general submission of the remaining Leinster rebels. But the rising was not yet completely over. French aid finally arrived on 27 August 1798 in the form of 1,000 Republican soldiers under the command of General Humbert. They landed in Killala Bay, bordering County Mayo and County Sligo. They were joined by mainly unarmed Irish volunteers and they defeated government military forces at Castlebar. Later, however, they were forced to surrender at Ballinamuck. One of Tone's brothers, Matthew, who was with Humbert's army, was tried and executed.

Later, *The Hoche*, one of several ships of the French fleet, arrived in Lough Swilly in County Donegal, but was forced to submit to English forces immediately on landing. Wolfe Tone, who was aboard, was taken prisoner and transported to Dublin where he was lodged in the Provost's prison (Arbour Hill). He knew that death awaited him and he asked to be shot like a soldier in deference to the uniform of a French officer which he wore. The decision of the court marshal, however, was that he was to be hanged like a common criminal.

In his speech from the dock Tone included the following remarks:

That Ireland was not able of herself to throw off the yoke, I knew. I therefore sought for aid wherever it was to be found. In honourable poverty, I rejected offers, which to a man in my circumstances, might be considered advantageous. I remained faithful to what I thought the cause of my country and sought in the French Republic an ally, to rescue three million of my countrymen from ...

Here the judge intervened and refused to allow him to continue this line of argument. Tone continued:

As to the connection between this country and Great Britain, I repeat it – all that has been imputed to me, words, writings, and actions I here deliberately avow. I have spoken and acted with reflection, and on principle, and am ready to meet the consequences. Whatever the sentence of this court, I am prepared for it. Its members will surely discharge their duty. I shall take care not to be wanting in mine.

Tone also paid tribute to the Catholics of Ireland:

When the friends of my youth swarmed off to leave me alone, the Catholics did not desert me. They had the virtue even to sacrifice their own interests to a rigid principle of honour.

After sentencing, Tone wrote two letters to his wife. In the first one he said:

> The hour is at last come when we must part. As no words can express what I feel for you and our children, I shall not attempt it; complaint of any kind would be beneath your courage and mine; be assured I will die as I have lived and you will have no cause to blush for me ... above all things, remember that you are now the only parent of our dearest children, and the best proof you can give of your affection for me, will be to preserve yourself for their education. God Almighty bless you all.

His second letter included the following words: 'Adieu, dearest love. Keep your courage as I have kept mine; my mind is as tranquil this moment as at any period of my life. Cherish my memory, and especially, preserve your health and spirit for the sake of our dearest children.'

He died in prison on 19 November 1798 in mysterious circumstances. Some contended that, rather than suffer the indignity of being hanged, he took his own life; others maintained that he was poisoned. The report issued by the British military was that a sentry found Tone in his cell with a deep wound across his neck. A surgeon stopped the flow of blood. Tone died seven days later. He was only thirty-five years of age. No one was allowed near him except the surgeon and the guards. No relatives were permitted to visit the dying man. No coroner's inquest was held. The contention that he committed suicide, it might be argued, was contrary to his frame of mind as expressed in both his penultimate and final letters to his wife.

Tone's body was handed over to his father. No funeral was allowed, and only two men were allowed to travel with the coffin to the family burial plot at Bodenstown, County Kildare.

The rising was now truly over.

THE AFTERMATH OF THE RISING

Death of Grattan

Henry Grattan was not a Member of Parliament during the 1798 Rising. He later became a member of the British House of Commons after the Act of Union. He died in London on 4 June 1820. He had expressed a wish to be buried in Moyanna, near Vicarstown in County Laois, but his peers decided that Westminster Abbey in London was a more fitting location and so it is here that his remains lie.

Among many of Henry Grattan's attributes is that of conservationist of the natural environment. On one occasion, a friend visiting him at his Wicklow home pointed out that a large beech tree was dangerously near his house. Grattan replied, 'Yes, I have often thought that I must have the house moved.'

The Act of Union, 1801

The English view of Ireland was that a formal union with Great Britain was the only safe way of maintaining English imperial control. Also to be avoided, at all costs, was the possibility in the future of rebellious elements in Ireland receiving French aid again. It was thought, too, that the Church of Ireland (Anglican), threatened by three quarters of the population, could be made secure only by a union of the two State churches. By rampant bribery and corruption, members of the Irish Parliament agreed to the Parliament's demise and, so, in January 1799, it held its last session.

In January 1800, the Parliament met in London and the terms of the union were confirmed. The bill for the 'United Kingdom of Great Britain and Ireland' received royal assent in 1 August. On 1 January 1801, the act came into being.

Ireland was now again securely held in place by Britain – for the present.

Wolfe Tone's grave at Bodenstown, County Kildare.

TONE'S GRAVE
Thomas Davis
– Excerpt –

In Bodenstown churchyard there is a green grave,
And wildly along it the winter winds rave;
Small shelter, I ween, are the ruined walls there
When the storm sweeps down on the plains of Kildare.

Once I lay on that sod – it lies over Wolfe Tone –
And thought how he perished in prison alone,
His friends unavenged, and his country unfreed –
'Oh! bitter,' I said, 'is the patriot's meed!' ...

In Bodenstown churchyard there is a green grave,
And freely around it let winter winds rave;
Far better they suit him – the ruin and the gloom –
Till Ireland, a nation, can build him a tomb.

Chapter 6

THE 1803 RISING

PRINCIPAL CHARACTERS

ROBERT EMMET
  Leader of the Rising
THOMAS RUSSELL
  Fellow Revolutionary
ANNE DEVLIN
  Fellow Revolutionary
MICHAEL DWYER
  Leader of Guerrilla Campaign
SARAH CURRAN
  Fiancée of Robert Emmet
LORD KILWARDEN
  Lord Chief Justice of Ireland
GENERAL JOSEPH HOLT
  A Leader of the Rising

BACKGROUND

With the Act of Union in 1801 the Kingdom of Ireland came to an end and the political connection with England was cemented in the English legal entity known as the United Kingdom of Great Britain and Ireland. What remained then in Dublin was the office of viceroy, a privy council (a body of advisers to the sovereign) the Established Church (Anglican), the judiciary and a few necessary officials. Dublin city, once a grand stately capital, now gradually fell in status to that of a provincial city.

The new legal entity in which the country now found itself was brought into effect without the native Irish people having any say in the matter. To make matters worse, the British failed to carry out either the promise of allowing full Catholic emancipation or the settlement of the tithe question. These matters, together with that of Irish self-government, continued to be blocked by the British House of Lords. In general, Ireland, as regards the native Irish at least, fell into a state of apathy. An exception to this, however, was the continuing resistance to British domination by rebels who survived the oppression which continued in the aftermath of the 1798 Rising. These, however, were few in number and were largely confined to the area of the Wicklow hills for tactical and safety reasons.

Robert Emmet

> Robert Emmet – the young, the ardent, the devoted Emmet! What emotion does not mention of the revered name call forth? Beloved it is by every true 'Son of Erin'; honoured by Britons; and consecrated as something holy in the 'heart of hearts' of each worshipper at the shrine of freedom.
>
> — *Memoir of Robert Emmet*, H. O'Neill, circa 1830

Robert Emmet was born in Molesworth Street, Dublin, on 4 March 1778. Shortly afterwards, his family moved to 109 St Stephen's Green in Dublin. His family was Protestant and well known in the area. His father, a doctor from Tipperary town, served as a surgeon to the Lord Lieutenant of Ireland and to members of the British royal family on their visits to Ireland. Emmet's mother was Elizabeth Mason from Ballydowney, Killarney, County Kerry.

Emmet was educated at a primary school run by the Edward brothers in Dropping's Court in Dublin (off Golden Lane) and later at the English Grammar School in Grafton Street. It may have been in the latter school that Emmet came under the influence of a Reverend Lewis, a Protestant minister, who inculcated in the young boy in an exceptionally deep way the principles of truth and justice.

At the age of sixteen, Emmet entered Trinity College, Dublin. He showed a particular proficiency in chemistry and mathematics, and also distinguished himself as an orator in the Historical Society. He developed an interest in politics and, in due course, became one of the leaders of the secret committee of the United Irishmen in the College.

However, evidently it was not secret enough and his membership culminated in his having to leave the college in 1798. Undoubtedly, Emmet was greatly influenced in his republican ideas by his elder brother, Thomas Addis Emmet, a close friend of Wolfe Tone. Tone was a frequent visitor to the house when Robert was growing up. As with many others, Emmet was influenced, too, by French revolutionary principles. Suspecting that he was about to be arrested for his political views, he travelled to France in 1800 as a United Irishmen emissary and he remained there until 1802. In that year, he led a delegation to Napoleon to seek aid for a rising set for August of the following year. This was intended to coincide with an expected invasion by Napoleon of England at that time. However, help was not forthcoming from the French and Emmet returned to Ireland in October 1802 to prepare for what would now be a self-financing rising. There was, apparently, still an expectation in Emmet's mind that the French would invade England sometime in the second half of 1803.

Statue of Robert Emmet, St Stephen's Green, Dublin. Sculptor: Jerome Connor.

Sarah Curran

During 1798, Emmet met Sarah Curran, a sister of fellow university student Richard Curran. Emmet fell in love with her. It was said that the couple met at a dance in Wicklow. Sarah's father, John Philpot Curran, a well-known lawyer, strongly opposed the relationship. Nevertheless, Robert and Sarah became secretly engaged sometime before July 1803.

Michael Dwyer

Michael Dwyer was born in the townland of Camara, in the Glen of Imaal, County Wicklow in 1772. He joined the United Irishmen in 1798 and was actively engaged in that rising under the command of General Joseph Holt. He also took part in battles at Arklow, Vinegar Hill, Ballyellis and Hacketstown. Following the failure of the 1798 Rising, Dwyer took to the hills, still under General Holt's leadership, and from the relative safety of the Wicklow Mountains he conducted a guerrilla campaign. The British put a price on his head and that, together with harsh treatment carried against anyone thought to have harboured him, eventually led to his being captured in December 1803. But before this in February 1799, when the cottage in which he was hiding was surrounded by British soldiers, one of his number who was already wounded, Sam Mc Allister, stood in the doorway and took the gunfire on himself, thereby allowing Dwyer to escape.

Previously, Dwyer and Emmet had met, but Dwyer was reluctant to allow his followers to engage in the 1803 Rising unless some indications were forthcoming that a measure of success was assured. This not being the case, he opted out of assisting Emmet.

Following the capture of Dwyer, he was transported to Australia, where he died in 1825.

Michael Dwyer's cottage, Glen of Imaal, County Wicklow.

Thomas Russell

Thomas Russell was born in Dromahane, County Cork, in 1767 to an Anglican family. He served with the British army in India and returned to Ireland in 1790. Here, like many others, he was influenced by the French Revolution, and this led to his taking an active part in organising the Society of United Irishmen. His activities landed him in jail during the 1798 Rising. Russell's endeavours to organise actions in the north in conjunction with the proposed 1803 Rising found little support. He, thus, fled to Dublin, where he was arrested and sent to Downpatrick Gaol in County Down. There, he was executed by beheading on 21 October 1803.

THE 1803 RISING

Due to an explosion of powder stores in a United Irishmen depot in Patrick Street, Dublin on 16 July 1803, the plan for a possible rising was exposed. Emmet was, consequently, forced to prematurely commence the rising.

The plan of action drawn up by Emmet included an initial attack on Dublin Castle and also on the batteries and stores held at the

Pigeon House fort at the mouth of Dublin Port. These actions were to be undertaken with the assistance of working people (who had been active in the 1798 Rising) from the counties of Wicklow and Wexford, who, traditionally in the months of June and July, came in considerable numbers to the neighbourhood of Dublin for the purpose of haymaking. However, for reasons that are not clear, on the day before this proposed action, 22 July 1803, they decided against taking part.

The failure of this first step of the proposed action to mature must have been dispiriting for Emmet. A note composed by him in his 'depot' in Butterfield Lane in Rathfarnham after this news ran as follows:

> I have little time to look at the thousand difficulties which still lie between me and the completion of my wishes, that those difficulties will, likewise, disappear, I have ordered and I trust, rational hopes [*sic*]; but if it is not to be the case, I thank God for having gifted me with a sanguine disposition; to that disposition I run for reflection; and if my hopes are without foundation – if a precipice is opened under my feet, from which duty will not suffer me to run back, I am grateful for the sanguine disposition which leads me to the brink and throws me down, while my eyes are raised to the vision of happiness that my fancy formed in the air.

Emmet was undoubtedly acutely aware that the United Irishmen organisation was well infiltrated by spies. Consequently, he tried to ensure that fewer persons be admitted into the confidence of the leaders of the planned rising. The disadvantage of this policy, however, meant that it was hardly surprising that those who knew little or nothing beforehand of what was planned should not be willing, when the rising commenced, to follow without question where they might be led and to obey the orders of almost unknown commanders.

There was to be further disappointment for Emmet, also on 22 July. Three hundred volunteers from Kildare, after marching into the capital, were persuaded by their leaders to disband and return home. Their failure to join in the rising was due to a lack of confidence in Emmet; most of them had never seen him before, and they were struck by his tender years and considered that he could not have sufficient military experience to lead them. Additionally, they were unimpressed by the quality of arms available to them, mainly pikes and a meagre supply of guns. They further considered that it would be necessary for French aid to arrive first before they would be prepared to join in the action. Nothing daunted, Emmet carried on with the proposed rising.

On 23 July, one of Emmet's supporters described what then occurred as follows:

At 8 p.m. precisely we sallied forth out of the depot; and when we arrived in Thomas Street the insurgents gave three deafening cheers. The consternation excited by our presence defies description. Every avenue emptied its curious hundreds, and almost every window exhibited half a dozen inquisitive heads, while peaceable shopkeepers ran to their doors, and beheld with amazement a lawless band of armed insurgents, in the midst of a peaceable city, an hour, at least, before dark. The scene at first might have appeared amusing to a careless spectator from the singular and dubious character which the riot wore; but when the rocket ascended and burst over the heads of the people, the aspect of things underwent an immediate and wonderful change. The impulse of the moment was self preservation; and those who, a few moments before, seemed to look on with vacant wonder, now assumed a face of horror, and fled with precipitation. The wish to escape was simultaneous: only the eagerness with which the people retreated from before us impeded their flight, as they crowded upon one another in the entrance to alleys, court-ways, and lanes, while the screams of woman and children were frightful and heart rending.

'To the Castle!' cried our enthusiastic leader, drawing his sword, and his followers appeared to obey – but when we reached the Market-house, our adherents had wonderfully diminished, there not being more than twenty insurgents with us.

'Fire the rocket,' cried Malachy.

'Hold awhile,' said Emmet, snatching the match from the man's hand who was about applying it. 'Let no lives be unnecessarily lost, run back and see what detains the men.'

Malachy obeyed; and we remained near the Market-house, waiting their arrival, until the soldiers approached.

On their way through Thomas Street, however, some of Emmet's supporters came across Lord Chief Justice, Lord Kilwarden, who was passing through in his coach. They dragged him from the coach and wounded him so badly that he died a short time later.

Emmet had previously drawn up a proclamation entitled 'The Provisional Government to the People of Ireland' which was posted on Dublin walls. This document advocated the following sentiment: 'We fight that all of us may have our country, and, that done, each of us shall have his religion.'

The opening paragraph read as follows:

You are now called on to show to the world that you are competent to take your own place among the nations, that you have a right to claim their cognizance of you as an independent country, by the satisfactory proof you can furnish of your capability of maintaining your independence, your wrestling it from England with your own hands.

The rising was, not surprisingly, a failure. This was due to the lack of proper organisation, the fact that Ireland was still held down by a large army, and by the strong provisions of an Insurrection Act. The purpose of the Insurrection Act of 1796 was to 'suppress insurrection and prevent disturbance of the public peace'. The provisions of the act were widespread and included that those who were deemed to be in any way involved in illegal activities:

> whether he shall take such an oath, or enter into such engagement, or not, being by due course of law convicted thereof, shall be adjudged guilty of felony, and suffer death without benefit of clergy and every person who shall take such an oath or engagement not being hereto compelled by inevitable necessity, and being by due course of law thereof convicted, shall be adjudged guilty of felony and transported for life.

Emmet now managed to escape to the Wicklow Mountains. Before doing so he addressed his followers with these words:

> The justice of our cause must one day triumph, and let us not indiscreetly protract the period by any premature endeavours to accelerate it ... In revolts, the first blow decides the contest; we have aimed one and missing the mark, let us retire unobserved and leave the enemy ignorant of the hand which was raised for their destruction ... Let me, therefore, my friends, advise you to act with that prudence which becomes men engaged in the grandest of all causes – the liberation of their country ... but above all, never forget that you are United Irishmen! sworn to promote the liberty of your country by all the means in your power ... Over my future destiny Fate has thrown a veil which mortal eyes cannot penetrate. Should I succeed in evading the pursuit of my enemies, you may expect to see me once more armed in the cause of Ireland but should I fall on the scaffold, let not the coward or the knave intimidate you from again and again appealing to Heaven on behalf of your rights and liberties by appealing to my recent failure.

Wanting desperately to see Sarah Curran, Emmet moved back to his old lodgings in Harold's Cross in Dublin. In the course of trying to see her over a period of one month he was one day surrounded in his house by police officers, headed by Major Sirr, and taken prisoner.

The final paragraph of a letter written by Emmet to Sarah Curran in September 1803 reads as follows:

> I have written to your father to come to me tomorrow. Had you not better speak to himself tonight? Destroy my letters that there may be nothing against yourself, and deny having any knowledge of me further than seeing me once or twice. For God's sake, write to me by the bearer one line to tell me how you are in spirits. I have no anxiety, no care, about myself; but am terribly oppressed about you. My dearest love, I would with joy lay down my life, but ought I do more? Do not be alarmed; they may try to frighten you; but they cannot do more. God bless you, my dearest love.
>
> I must send this off at once; I have written it in the dark. My dearest Sarah, forgive me.

Anne Devlin

Anne Devlin was born in Rathdrum, County Wicklow in the year 1780. Following the rising of 1798 she and her family were the subject of many raids by the authorities. Her family moved to Dublin in 1800 and it was here that she met Robert Emmet who was based in nearby Butterfield Lane, in Rathfarnham. In order to avoid undue suspicion of the constant activities going on in his house, Emmet asked Anne to act as a housekeeper to give an air of normalcy to his abode. After the failure of the rising, the local military raided the house and arrested Anne and her eight-year-old sister. While incarcerated Anne was subjected to the torture of half-hanging, but refused to provide any information about Emmet. The family returned to their home in Rathfarnham but later the entire family was seized by the military. Anne was interrogated by Major Sirr but again refused to provide any information about Emmet. She was then sent to Kilmainham Gaol, where she was threatened with death. Emmet himself was also lodged in Kilmainham at this time and urged her to inform on him as his fate was already a foregone conclusion. She refused to do so. She was released in 1806. She later married but apparently died in poverty in the Liberties of Dublin in 1851.

The Trial of Robert Emmet

Emmet was tried at Green Street Court, Dublin, by a special commission. He was 'defended' by a man named Leonard Mc Nally who, it was later discovered, was a spy and in the pay of the government.

Green Street Courthouse, Dublin.

Emmet was charged with high treason and found guilty. His speech from the dock was remarkable in its courage and became an inspiration for future generations of Irish men and women. An excerpt of it is given here:

> My country was my idol. To it I sacrificed every selfish, every endearing sentiment; and for it I now offer up myself, O God!

I acted as an Irishman, determined on delivering my country from the yoke of a foreign and unrelenting tyranny, and the more galling yoke of a domestic faction, which is its joint partner and perpetrator in the patricide, from the ignominy existing with an exterior of splendour and a conscious depravity. It was the wish of my heart to extricate my country from this doubly riveted despotism. I wished to place her independence beyond the reach of any power on earth. I wished to exalt her to that proud station in the world. Connection with France was, indeed, intended, but only as far as mutual interest would sanction or require. Were the French to assume any authority inconsistent with the purest independence, it would be the signal for their destruction. We sought their aid and we sought it as we had assurance we should obtain it, as auxiliaries in war and allies in peace.

The most notable quotation from his speech was:

I am going to my cold and silent grave: my lamp of life is nearly extinguished: my race is run: the grave opens to receive me, and I sink into its bosom! I have but one request to ask at my departure from this world – it is the charity of its silence! Let no man write my epitaph: for as no man who knows my motives dare now vindicate them, let not prejudice or ignorance asperse them. Let them and me repose in obscurity and peace, and my tomb remain uninscribed, until other times, and other men, can do justice to my character, when my country takes her place among the nations of the earth, then, and not till then, let my epitaph be written. I have done.

The speech became required reading for aspiring orators in the years ahead. It was said that Abraham Lincoln memorised it in its entirety.

The poet Thomas Moore, a contemporary of the times, said of Emmet:

> Were I to number the men above all I have ever known who appeared to me to combine in the greatest degree pure oral worth with intellectual power, I should, have among the highest of the few placed Robert Emmet.

Later, W.B. Yeats described Emmet as: 'Foremost amongst Saints of Nationality.'

On 20 September 1803, Robert Emmet was hanged and beheaded outside St Catherine's Church in Thomas Street, Dublin. He was twenty-five years of age. Of the nineteen rebels found guilty of participating in the rising, seventeen were executed.

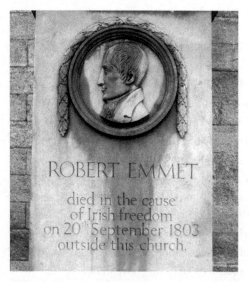

Plaque commemorating the execution of Robert Emmet at St Catherine's Church, Thomas Street, Dublin.

Comments of an admirer (but not an active supporter) of Emmet stated in the *Dublin and London Magazine* of 1825:

116

[H]e died as he lived, with heroic fearlessness and decent fortitude. The amiable, though enthusiastic Emmet, however, we hope, has not died in vain. Our rulers must learn from his history, that a people without confidence, is a moral Hydra, never to be deprived of the means of doing mischief. The head of one Rebellion is no sooner lopped off, than another is generated. The Hercules, who is to annihilate the monster, can only be found in that act of wisdom and justice, which is to reconcile the people to their rulers by making them freemen ... The fate of Robert Emmet demanded something more than tears; and unprofitable as these may have been, we have continued to offer them still to his memory. But let our private sorrows pass – history, one day, will do him justice. I have thrown my mite into the scale, in which his reputation yet trembles; and, inadequate as that may be, it is sincere and impartial. All ye who knew him in his 'hour of pride', go and do likewise.

Sarah Curran, still disowned by her father because of her liaison with Emmet, later married a Captain Sturgeon, a nephew of the Marquis of Rockingham. They had one child whose early death impacted adversely on Sarah's own health. She died in Kent in 1808, still disowned by her father to the extent that he refused to allow her to be interred with her sister in the grounds of the family home in Rathfarnham in Dublin.

Robert Emmet's last wish that he be allowed to 'repose in obscurity' did indeed come to pass. The whereabouts of his remains are a mystery. It was thought that, perhaps, he had been buried secretly in a vault of a Dublin Anglican church, or in the now demolished St Peter's Church in Aungier Street or in St Michan's Church in Church Street, Dublin, but the matter remains a mystery.

One does not have to hate one's enemy to love one's country.

— *Robert Emmet*

Chapter 7

THE YOUNG IRELAND RISING

1848

PRINCIPAL CHARACTERS

THOMAS DAVIS
   Founder of Young Ireland
WILLIAM SMITH O'BRIEN
   Leader of Young Ireland
JOHN MITCHELL
   Founder of *The United Irishman* newspaper
DANIEL O'CONNELL
   Promoter of Catholic Emancipation
JAMES FINTAN LALOR
   Young Ireland Supporter

BACKGROUND

The political and social state of Ireland after the 'Emmet' rising of 1803 was greatly affected by a number of factors. One of these was the introduction of further Insurrection Acts. From 1833 a new type of Coercion Act was passed as a standard response to Irish disorders. Under this act, trial by magistrates was replaced by trial by military courts. The imposition of the new act was accompanied by ongoing resistance to British rule as evidenced by, for example, the activities of William Smith O'Brien. The second and even more significant factor was the impact of the Famine.

The Famine, 1845–1849
In 1851 the census showed the population at 6.5 million. However, the projected normal growth rate of the population, based on the 1841 census, indicated that the figure should have been in the region of 9 million. Consequently, about 2.5 million people had 'disappeared'. Of these, approximately 1.5 million emigrated and about 1 million died of starvation. Before this, in 1845, the population, except for some industrialised parts of the north-east of the country, was dependant on agriculture. Remarkably, the very survival of the native population

depended almost solely on one crop: the potato.

The plight of the Irish peasant was such that they lived in squalid conditions on a tiny plot of land for which they had to pay a high rent to their aristocratic landlord. In order to pay the rent, they had to sell cereal crops and subsist on the produce from what tiny space of ground was left for growing potatoes. If they could not pay the rent, they were evicted.

The British government was aware of the possible consequences of the dependence on the potato crop by what was then an increasing population in Ireland. A government commission in 1845 reported:

> If the present trend towards subdivision [of small plots of land between family members] continues and the present reliance on the potato continues among the peasantry, calamity would seem an almost inevitable consequence.

For the government, however, the overriding principle was that the economic dictum of laissez-faire be allowed to rule in all circumstances. To intervene in Ireland's economy would be to interfere with natural economic developments. Additionally, Ireland was never a primary concern of the British government – neither Prime Minister Russell nor Prime Minister Peel visited Ireland during this most appalling crisis in her history.

Some landlords and other groups did their best to alleviate the suffering. For example, the Quakers (Society of Friends) set up soup kitchens throughout the country. It was clear from the outset, however, that if the potato crop were to fail the results would be dire. And dire they proved to be. A fine sunny summer in 1845 was brought to an end by showers of sleet, thunder and lightening and heavy rain. This weather was conducive to the propagation and spread of potato blight (fungus phytophthora infestans) resulting in tubers simply rotting in the ground. The blight struck with alarming speed, potatoes being ruined within a matter of days. By the beginning of 1846 the blight had struck every county of Ireland.

Detail of the monument to the memory of the victims of the Great Famine, Custom House Quay, Dublin. Sculptor: Rowan Gillespie.

The British government, under Sir Robert Peel, ordered maize (Indian corn) from America which was to be sold in Ireland at low cost. The imported corn was not released immediately for consumption, but rather issued piecemeal in order to control prices. Import merchants, on hearing of the provision of cheap food, almost immediately halted their import activities fearing financial loss. The result of this was that the government was the sole provider of food for the entire native population of Ireland, a task it was unable to meet.

The second action of the government was to set up a relief commission. Under its provisions public works were instituted which allowed labourers to earn money to buy food. However, the scheme had only limited success, although the numbers employed had reached three quarters of a million in 1847. Corruption in the handling of funds was one of the limiting factors.

The government's third action was to repeal the Corn Laws which had provided protectionist duties on grain. The purpose of this action, ultimately, was to reduce the cost of bread – but this was of little use to most, who could not afford bread at any price. While the native Irish were starving, food was being exported, with every other crop, apart from the potato, enjoying a successful harvest.

Workhouses were set up but the numbers who could avail themselves of these was relatively small; this, together with those reliant on public works, still left about 1.5 million people without means to survive. Workhouses, funded as they were by taxes paid by landlords and major farmers, were made as uncomfortable as possible to discourage their use, thereby relieving the level of taxes necessary to run them.

Mass emigration, mainly to the United States, ensued. Many boat passengers never got to their destination, dying en route in the most atrocious conditions.

'The Dunbrody' replica emigrant ship berthed at New Ross.

The use of the Irish language declined significantly after the Great Famine. This was largely because it became associated with a Celtic past of dire poverty and, additionally, it was clear that the English language would be needed by the waves of emigrants who would leave Ireland's shores forever. It could be said, then, that Ireland's heart was knocked out of her for many decades after the Famine.

Catholic Emancipation

Daniel O'Connell was born near Cahirciveen, County Kerry on 6 August 1775. His family background was unusual for the times in that he hailed from a Catholic aristocratic tradition. The O'Connells were landlords but kept a low political profile. O'Connell's first language growing up was Irish. He was educated in Ireland and France. In 1794 he entered Lincoln's Inn (UK) and was called to the Bar in Dublin in 1798.

Daniel O'Connell, MP. Engraving by William Holl II. © National Gallery of Ireland.

O'Connell practised law until 1823. In that year, he founded the Catholic Association with the aim of seeking Catholic emancipation through constitutional means. Using his extraordinary powers of oratory he toured the country, rallying the people and raising a 'Fighting Fund' by charging a penny a month membership fee. In 1824, he was imprisoned for a 'seditious' address to the people of Ireland. In 1828, he was elected to the British Parliament after defeating the government candidate in County Clare. In the election he was well supported by the Catholic clergy, whose influence on the poor peasant class was enormous. However, he was debarred from taking his seat in Parliament as Catholics were prescribed from doing so unless they agreed to abjure certain basic tenets of the Catholic religion.

Due to O'Connell's huge following and fearing an insurrection, the British government, under the then prime minister, the Duke of Wellington, granted Catholic emancipation in 1829; thus, in February of 1830, Daniel O'Connell became the first Catholic in modern history to sit in the British House of Commons. However, the granting of emancipation and its consequent voting rights were subsequently countered by the British government by their passing a Disenfranchisement Act. Due to this act the level of wealth necessary to qualify for a vote, already way beyond the reach of most people, was raised substantially, with the result that the Irish electorate was reduced to a mere 16,000 votes.

Later, O'Connell formed the Repeal Association with the aim of repealing the Act of Union with Britain by the same peaceful means he had applied to obtaining Catholic emancipation. He organised 'monster rallies'. On one occasion, as many as three quarters of a million people gathered on the Hill of Tara to hear the man they called 'The Liberator'. He was arrested and charged with conspiracy and sentenced to a year in prison, but he served only three months. In 1841, he was elected Lord Mayor of Dublin.

O'Connell abhorred violence. This probably stemmed, firstly, from a reported duel in 1815 in which his opponent died and, secondly, from the influence on him of the turbulence of the French Revolution.

In 1846, the Repeal Association became split because many of its younger members had become impatient with the Liberator's constitutional methods, which appeared to be yielding little fruit. Those who were dissatisfied were Young Irelanders, and they now formed the Irish Confederation, an organisation that was prepared to countenance the use of violence to achieve Irish freedom.

O'Connell Monument, O'Connell Street, Dublin. Sculptor: John Henry Foley.

Meanwhile, the plight of the general population remained desperate. This is illustrated in the following excerpt from a written address by O'Connell to a Repeal Association meeting held in Conciliation Hall, in Dublin's Burgh Quay. It was reported about in the *Evening Mail* of 29 June 1846. Referring to the depravation of agricultural labourers O'Connell said:

It is not possible for the Irish people to endure their misery much longer. I, who detest anything revolutionary, and abhor violent changes, and would not take the best amelioration of public institutions at the expense of a single drop of blood, tell you that the people of Ireland, cannot much longer endure their present misery.

These sentiments were expressed by O'Connell even before the full effects of famine manifested themselves.

With support waning, O'Connell left for Rome for health reasons. He died en route at Genoa on 15 May 1847. His body is buried in Glasnevin Cemetery in Dublin and his heart is buried in Rome.

William Smith O'Brien

William Smith O'Brien was born on 17 October 1803 at Dromolond Castle, County Clare and was a direct descendant of Brian Boru on his father's side. An aristocratic Protestant landlord, he was elected Conservative Member of Parliament at Westminster for County Limerick in 1835, having previously been a Member of Parliament for Ennis, County Clare. Initially, he had an uneasy relationship with Daniel O'Connell, the leader of the Catholic Association. However, Smith O'Brien later became a tireless advocate of Catholic Emancipation, although he disagreed with O'Connell's view that violence could never be justified in the pursuit of freedom. Later, this led to O'Brien becoming the leader of the Irish Confederation, the breakaway group of Young Irelanders from O'Connell's Repeal Association.

William Smith O'Brien. 'Young Irelander in Kilmainham Gaol' by Irish nineteenth-century engraver Henry O'Neill. © National Gallery of Ireland.

Thomas Davis and 'Young Ireland'

The title 'Young Ireland' was given to a nationalist movement, founded in 1840, by Thomas Davis. Davis was born in Mallow, County Cork on 14 October 1814. He was brought up in the Protestant faith and received his education at Mr Mungan's School in Lower Mount Street in Dublin. He graduated from Trinity College in 1836 and was called to the Irish Bar a year later.

Statue of Thomas Davis, College Green, Dublin. Sculptor: Edward Delaney.

The Young Irelanders' aim was, like O'Connell's, to gain repeal of the union with Britain, but its methods were, in many ways, opposed to those of O'Connell. They sought to instil in the Irish people a sense of national identity by reminding them of the days of their past glories – the days of the Fianna with their noble ideals, of the days of saints and scholars. They wished to revive the native language of the country, now falling into disuse, and to revive old Gaelic stories and legends. Davis expressed his views on the Irish language in the following comments:

A people without a language of its own is only half a nation;
To lose your native language and learn that of an alien is the
worst badge of conquest – it is the chain on the soul ... A nation
should guard its language more than its territories, it being a
surer barrier. Should they abandon this for the mongrel of a
hundred breeds called English?

Davis was a poet and a writer. In 1841, he founded the profoundly
influential and radical newspaper *The Nation* and contributed many
articles to it. The newspaper was a major success and enjoyed a wide
circulation throughout the country. Co-founders of the newspaper
were Charles Gavin Duffy and John Blake Dillon. Davis died at the
early age of thirty in September of 1845 from scarlet fever.

Also hugely influential in the Irish Confederation was James
Fintan Lalor. This County Laois man was renowned for his powerful
writings and he, too, contributed to *The Nation* newspaper. He took an
active part in the rising. He suffered from ill health all his life and was
partially crippled. He died, apparently from an attack of bronchitis,
on 27 December 1849.

THE YOUNG IRELAND RISING

With the conviction that the Irish Members of Parliament at Westminster were wasting their time in pursuing Irish interests by political
means, in 1848 Smith O'Brien organised and participated in an armed
rising. His aide-de-camp was James Stephens, a Young Ireland supporter. They were probably spurred on by revolutionary activities in
Europe such as the collapse of the French monarchy (Louis Philippe),
the struggle of Hungary against Austria and the rising of individual
states in Italy against their rulers. However, in Ireland, probably due
to the effects of the Famine, there was little interest in the country
for an armed struggle. Nevertheless, in July of that year a small group
under Smith O'Brien clashed with a small force of policemen in Ballingarry, County Tipperary, but were unsuccessful. Smith O'Brien was

arrested, found guilty of high treason and sentenced to be hanged. The sentence was commuted to 'permanent exile' and in 1849 he was transported to Tasmania, then known as Van Diemen's Island. He later managed to return to Ireland, where he died in 1864.

In the abortive rising, Smith O'Brien was joined by John Mitchell. Mitchell was the son of a Presbyterian minister from Ulster. In 1840, Mitchell abandoned his law practice and concentrated on writing articles for *The Nation* newspaper. He joined its staff in 1845. His articles made very clear his total opposition to English rule in Ireland. In 1848 he became dissatisfied with the Young Irelanders and founded his own newspaper, *The United Irishman*. It was an article in this paper that led to his being arrested and eventually being found guilty of the charge of treason felony. He was condemned to fourteen years' transportation to Tasmania. His speech from the dock commenced with the following words:

The law has now done its part, and the Queen of England, her crown and Government in Ireland, are now secure pursuant to Act of Parliament. I have done my part also. Three months ago I promised Lord Clarendon [Lord Lieutenant and Governor General of Ireland], and his government, in this country, that I would provoke him into his courts of justice, as places of this kind are called, and that I would force him publicly and notoriously to pack a jury against me to convict me, or else that if I would walk out a free man from this dock, to meet him in another field. My Lord, I knew I was setting my life on that cast; but I warned him that in either event the victory would be with me, and victory is with me. Neither the jury, nor the judges, nor any other man in this court, presumes to imagine that it is a criminal who stands in this dock. I have kept my word. I have shown what the law is made of in Ireland. I have shown that her Majesty's Government sustains itself in Ireland by packed juries, by partisan judges, by perjured sheriffs. I have acted all through this business, from the first, under a strong sense of duty. I do not repent anything I have done and I believe that the course which I have opened is only commenced ...

Statue of John Mitchell, John Mitchell Place off Main Street, Newry. County Down.

Wexford man Thomas Francis Meagher also participated in the rising and was exiled to Australia. He eventually escaped to America, where he became a prominent figure in the New York political and legal circles. Gavin Duffy was also deported.

After the Young Ireland Rising had been repressed, there followed a period of relative quiet. However, persistent discontent among the native Irish population remained. Cases of eviction were common and tenants still had to contend with very high rents, no fixity of tenure and no compensation for improvements to their holdings made by the tenant.

Although the 1848 Rising could barely justify the title of 'rising' (it also became known as the 'cabbage patch rebellion' because the escape route, taken by Smith O'Brien from the cottage he was in, was cultivated as a cabbage patch), it could be said that its importance lay in the fact that it sowed the seeds of the spirit of republicanism that was to develop into a wider and much more significant movement in later years.

Chapter 8

THE FENIAN RISING

1867

PRINCIPAL CHARACTERS

JAMES STEPHENS
   Founder of the IRB
THOMAS CLARKE LUBY
   Founder of the IRB
JOHN O'MAHONY
   Leader of the IRB
JOHN O'LEARY
   Member of the IRB
JEREMIAH O'DONOVAN ROSSA
   Member of the IRB
JOHN MITCHELL
   Leading Member of the Fenian Movement

BACKGROUND

In considering the background to the Fenian Rising it could be said that the aftermath of the impact of the Famine continued to have a significant effect. Additionally, the relatively short time lapse between the 1848 Rising and the 1867 Rising meant that republican ideals continued to develop; indeed, some of those who participated in the 1867 Rising, like James Stephens, John O'Leary and John Mitchell, had also taken part in the earlier one.

The Fenian Movement
In 1858, the Irish Republican Brotherhood (IRB) – an insurrectionary movement – was formed in Dublin by James Stephens and Thomas Clarke Luby. In the same year, a closely linked organisation was founded by John O'Mahony in New York called the Irish Revolutionary Brotherhood, later to be merged with the IRB. As a result of this American connection, thousands of emigrants who had been forced out of Ireland by the Great Famine and ended up in America, and many who had fought in the American Civil War (1861–1865), pledged to

return and fight for Ireland. The broad movement under which the nationalist cause was fostered became known as 'The Fenians'. The name was derived from the famous mythological 'Fianna' under their leader, Finn Mac Cool.

Thomas Clarke Luby was born in Dublin. His father was a Church of Ireland clergyman and his mother was a Catholic. He studied law in Trinity College, Dublin. After initially supporting O'Connell's Repeal Association, he joined the Young Irelanders and later became a member of the Fenian movement.

The Fenian views were reflected in their own newspaper entitled *Irish People*. Tipperary-born John O'Leary became editor of the newspaper. He had taken part in the abortive rising of 1848. He was arrested in 1865 and was sentenced to twenty years' penal servitude. He was released after five years, on condition that he stayed away from Ireland for the remaining period of his sentence. He lived in Paris until 1885, when he resettled in Dublin. He was against Parnell's Parliamentary Party at Westminster. By this time O'Leary was somewhat of a father figure to the nationalist movement. He died in 1907.

John Mitchell was of the upper echelons of the Fenian movement, as indicated in the previous chapter. He had escaped from his banishment to Tasmania and, in 1853, settled in New York. Here he founded a radical nationalist newspaper entitled *The Citizen*. Controversy arose, however, because of his expressed views in support of slavery and his associated racist views, as a result of which the paper ultimately failed. His view, that a rising against England while they were engaged in the Crimean War in 1854–1855 (England, France and Turkey versus Russia) would be opportune, was not supported by other Fenian leaders. His own enthusiasm for a rising then waned. He returned to Ireland in 1875 but died suddenly in that year.

There were two significant differences between the rising of 1867 and earlier risings. Firstly, in her struggle for freedom during the sixteenth and seventeenth centuries, Ireland had looked for help from Spain and France, but now, from about 1850 onwards, it was to her own exiled people in America that Ireland turned for aid. Secondly, the instigators of this latest rising came not so much from the middle/upper classes of Irish society, but rather from the ordinary citizens of the country.

Arms shipments from the United States were made to Ireland through Liverpool, and by 1865 arrangements seemed to be in place for a rising. However, the relations between Kilkenny-born James Stephens and his counterpart in America, John O'Mahony, broke down. Stephens constantly complained that the Fenian movement in America was not doing enough to supply him with arms and finance. O'Mahony apparently did not take kindly to the somewhat dictatorial attitude of Stephens. In the end, Stephens suspended the planned rising and declared that in the following year, 1866, he would personally lead a rising. However, he again decided not to proceed, and departed for France and later for America.

Prior to this Stephens had developed an idea, described by Pádraig Ó Concubhair in his book *The Fenians were Dreadful Men* (Mercier Press), as follows:

> that in the event of the establishment of an Irish Republic the example of America should be followed and a new capital city be created in the fashion of Washington DC, and this would be situated in Killarney where, he [Stephens] wrote, 'Our holiest love of Ireland was quickened by the shores of Loch Lein.'

Stephens was replaced as head of the Fenian movement by Colonel Thomas J. Kelly, who came to Ireland with a group of Irish-Americans for a rising now planned for 1867. Another important figure in the Fenian movement was Jeremiah O'Donovan Rossa. O'Donovan Rossa was born at Rosscarbery, County Cork, in September 1831. In 1856, he founded *The Phoenix National and Literary Society*, the aims of which were to support the liberation of Ireland by force of arms. The Society merged with the IRB two years later.

O'Donovan Rossa monument, St Stephen's Green, Dublin.

In 1858 O'Donovan Rossa was interned without trial on conspiracy charges. He was released after eight months but later, in 1865, he was accused of plotting a Fenian rising and imprisoned in England. In 1869, he was elected to the British House of Commons for the Tipperary constituency, beating off the challenge of a Liberal Catholic opponent. However, his election was declared invalid because he was an 'imprisoned felon'.

On his release from prison in 1871, O'Donovan Rossa was exiled to the USA, where he continued to support the Fenian movement.

THE FENIAN RISING

The first outbreak of the rising in Ireland was undertaken prematurely due to a breakdown in communications regarding a delivery of arms. It occurred in February 1867 in Cahirciveen, County Kerry, where a small rising took place following a gathering of insurgents at Ballycarberry Castle. Their intention was to march to Killarney for a planned rising there, but the work of an informer put a stop to it and, consequently, they made little or no progress.

Print of the town of Cahirciveen, County Kerry. 'The Illustrated London News',
2 March 1867.

Part of the accompanying report from the above-mentioned *Illustrated London News* read as follows:

There is no longer the slightest apprehension of any renewal of the late silly attempts of the Fenian conspirators to raise an insurrection in the county of Kerry. The presence of a whole division of British troops, under Sir Alfred Horsford, seems not only to have checked the advance of the Irish/American marauders, who are now reckoned at not more than fifty or a hundred men, but even to have scared them out of existence; for none can be found by the most assiduous beating of Toomies Wood and all the neighbouring coverts on the shores of the Lakes of Killarney.

In March other activities were carried out in several southern counties, including Cork (an attack at Fota near Cobh), Limerick (an attack on the barracks in Kilmallock and in the village of Ardagh), Clare, Waterford and Tipperary.

The views of the 'establishment' classes on these activities can be illustrated by the editorial of the *Cork Examiner* newspaper of 7 March 1867, part of which stated, in a somewhat exaggerated report:

With profound sorrow we have today to record the outbreak of an insane and criminal insurrection in the South of Ireland. The blow has fallen suddenly and unexpectedly. While the country was presenting the most peaceful aspect; while its criminal records seemed to indicate a steady, progressive improvement in the morals of the people, an absence of violence, a respect for law, a regard for the rights of property, affording ground for the most favourable auguries of the future of the country, there was concealed beneath the fair surface a vast mass of disaffection ready to break into open rebellion at the signal ... Three southern counties are wrapped from end to end in a flame of insurrection; sinister rumours reach us from all quarters that what has occurred is but a prelude to a still more extensive and formidable movement ... the movement is extensive and well organised – not the raid of a few desperate men, such as was seen a few days since in Kerry but a mature and deliberate attempt at revolution. That it has the slightest chance of attaining even a temporary success, a momentary advantage, no sane man will for a moment imagine, but we look forward with pain to the disastrous consequences to the country – the terrible retribution which the insurgents have drawn upon themselves, and which they will infallibly be made to suffer.

In Dublin about 1,000 men marched out of the city centre and made for the suburb of Tallaght. They captured a number of police barracks on the way. At Tallaght there were some slight skirmishes with the police, but all of these actions were speedily and easily suppressed by the authorities. Among the hundreds who were arrested and sentenced to long terms in jail was Thomas Clarke, later to be one of the signatories of the 1916 Proclamation.

The Fenian Insurrection: Conflict with the police, under Sub-Inspector Burke, at Tallaght, near Dublin. 'London Illustrated News', 16 March 1867.

The Fenian Rising was, additionally, badly affected by a major snowstorm, which lasted a number of days and impacted adversely on guerrilla warfare in particular.

The Manchester Martyrs

Three young Irishmen, Allen, Larkin and O'Brien, together with dozens of others were arrested following the successful freeing of two Fenians en route to jail in Manchester. In the course of the rescue, a policeman was shot dead, apparently accidentally, by a ricocheting bullet. The three men were found guilty of his murder and hanged in public on 23 November 1867. Although all three did take part in the rescue, none of them was guilty of the shooting. Many claims were made for the sentences to be reversed, but to no avail. Their hanging for a crime they did not commit caused a huge wave of sympathy in Ireland and in the many countries to which Irish people had emigrated, especially in the USA. Allen, Larkin and O'Brien became known as 'The Manchester Martyrs'.

London

On 13 December 1867 a small group of Fenians placed a barrel of gunpowder against the outer wall of Clerkenwell 'House of Detention' in London with the aim of freeing two Fenian prisoners. The impact of the resultant explosion was so great that not only was the wall of the prison blown open, but dozens of houses in the locality were destroyed or badly damaged. It was estimated that eighteen local people died and over a hundred were injured. Three of the Fenian instigators were captured but only one, Michael Barrett, received the death penalty for his actions. He was hanged on 26 May 1868. His was the last public hanging to be carried out in England.

Neither of the two Fenian prisoners escaped from the prison.

Support from America

The impact of the level of support in the USA for the Irish cause was evidenced by the fact that in 1866 an attempt was made to cross the US frontier and attack a British power base in Canada. The US government, after years of being both deaf and blind to Fenian activities, suddenly decided, possibly due to pressure from Britain, to take action by seizing arms and imprisoning many Fenian leaders. Two groups, however, did succeed in reaching Canadian territory. One group, under a Col. John O'Neill, with 1,400 men, defeated a troop of 'The Queens Own Volunteers' at Fort Erie, although O'Neill was later forced to surrender. The second group, from the State of Vermont, was forced back across the frontier by Canadian troops.

Conclusion

Hesitation by the leadership of the Fenians, together with the British government being alert to a possible rising, were major factors in the rising of 1867 being a failure. Even before the rising, such as it was, the British government learned through its spies that almost every ship that crossed the Atlantic from America brought to Ireland men of military experience.

The Fenian position was especially frustrated by the arrest of O'Leary, Luby and O'Donovan Rossa.

Despite the failure of the rising, there remained considerable support for Fenianism in Ireland – this notwithstanding the strong opposition to it by the Catholic Church. The Church was allegedly opposed to it because of its being a secret, oath-bound society. Fenianism was denounced from the altars and undoubtedly this had the effect of deterring very many Catholics from joining the organisation. However, Ireland was now a step closer to an even more significant rising.

Chapter 9

THE EASTER RISING

1916

PRINCIPAL CHARACTERS

PATRICK PEARSE
Leader of the Rising

JAMES CONNOLLY
Leader of the Rising

THOMAS J. CLARKE
Signatory of the 1916 Proclamation

SEÁN MAC DIARMADA
Signatory of the 1916 Proclamation

THOMAS MAC DONAGH
Signatory of the 1916 Proclamation

ÉAMONN CEANNT
Signatory of the 1916 Proclamation

JOSEPH MARY PLUNKETT
Signatory of the 1916 Proclamation

MICHAEL MALLIN
Leading supporter of the Rising

COUNTESS MARKIEVICZ
Leading Supporter of the Rising

ÉAMON DE VALERA
Leading Supporter of the Rising, and later Leader of Republican
Anti-Treaty forces

THOMAS KENT
Leading Supporter of the Rising

EDWARD DALY
Leading Supporter of the Rising

MICHAEL O'HANRAHAN
Leading Supporter of the Rising

CON COLBERT
Leading Supporter of the Rising

SÉAN HEUSTON
Leading Supporter of the Rising

WILLIE PEARSE
  Brother of Patrick Pearse and Supporter of the Rising

ROGER CASEMENT
  Humanitarian and Leading Supporter of Irish Freedom

W.T. COSGRAVE
  Participant in the 1916 Rising, and later Leader of the Pro-Treaty
  Free State Government

EOIN MAC NEILL
  Founder and Chief of Staff of the Irish Volunteers

BACKGROUND

It could be argued that at this stage in Ireland's history many Irish people had lost any hope of ridding themselves of the yoke of foreign domination. This was due, at least in part, to the cumulative impact of centuries of repression, copper-fastened by the sheer strength of the British Empire, together with the effects of the disastrous Famine during the period 1845–1849. The spark of independence was, however, about to be reignited in a way unforeseen by either the Irish people or their masters.

After the failure of the risings of 1848 and 1867, there was a period of relative calm, though this was still marked by considerable discontent among the native Irish population. Cases of eviction were common and tenants still had to put up with very high rents. Additionally, there was still no fixity of tenure. The impact of this continuing repression resulted in an unexpected outcome, namely, some English statesmen began to wonder if the Irish situation generally was in fact caused by their own actions. Because of this, an act was introduced by Prime Minister Gladstone for the disestablishment and disendowment of the 'Irish Church', i.e. the Church of Ireland. The Church of Ireland had now to be independent, self-supporting and financed by its own members. Disendowment meant that the government took over all remaining finances after providing for all those who held office in the Church. The surplus funds, amounting to several million pounds, were used partially to make grants to the Presbyterian Church and to the Catholic Maynooth College. This was done in order to enable these institutions, too, to become independent and self-supporting.

The government also now introduced, in 1870, the first Land Act. Under this act, a tenant could no longer be evicted as long as he paid his rent. Also, it was prescribed that an outgoing tenant should be compensated for improvements made by him. Although the act very much improved the position of the Irish tenants, the fixing of the level of rents was still in the landlords' hands; as such, the tenants' discontent continued, and was a prelude to the foundation of the Land League.

The Irish National Land League – Michael Davitt

The Land League was founded by Michael Davitt in 1879. The aims of the League were to prevent landlords from charging exorbitant rents and also to introduce a system whereby the government would provide finance to tenants for the purpose of their becoming owners of their holding. The tenants would then repay the government by easy instalments.

The method proposed by the Land League of dealing with landlords who were charging too high a rent was that the tenant, on being refused a reduction, should refuse to pay any rent. If evicted, and in the event of a new tenant moving in, the incoming tenant and his family were to be 'boycotted' – that is, none of the neighbours would have any contact with them, nor would any shopkeeper sell any goods to them. Furthermore, no one would buy any of their produce.

As often happens with 'political' movements of any kind, there are those who act outside the brief of the organisation. In this case, sometimes strong-arm tactics were adopted by way of paying off grudges and the Land League was blamed for these instances. In 1881, consequently, a new Coercion Bill was passed, under which the authorities would imprison any suspect for any length of time without trial.

The continuing discontentment of the population, however, again seemed to penetrate the upper echelons of the British Government and, in 1881, Gladstone's second Land Act was passed. Under this new act, Land Courts were set up to which a tenant could apply to have the rent lowered. In 1885, a third Land Act was passed, the effect of which was that a sum of money was made available to be loaned to Irish tenants to enable them to buy out their holding. This was the first step towards the eradication of Irish landlordism.

Charles Stewart Parnell and Home Rule

Charles Stewart Parnell was born on 27 June 1846 in County Wicklow. He was the seventh child and third son (there were eleven children in all) of an American mother, Delia Stewart, and John Henry Parnell, of Protestant stock, who had inherited Avondale House on a substantial estate in County Wicklow.

Portrait of Charles Stewart Parnell by the nineteenth-century Irish artist, Sydney Prior Hall. © National Gallery of Ireland.

Parnell received his early education in England and went up to Cambridge University in 1865. He was not overly studious and in 1869 he was 'sent down' for a period of two weeks as punishment for boisterous behaviour. As it was near the end of term, he decided not to return and instead to stay at home in Avondale. Here he soon developed a deep interest in Irish political matters, especially in relation to the downtrodden plight of the native Catholic populace. Parnell fully supported the ideals of the Land League and, in fact, became its first president.

In 1880, with the disastrous Famine of 1845–1849 still fresh in the memory of those who survived it, near famine conditions again prevailed and Parnell spent over two months in the USA canvassing for funds for famine relief and for the Land League.

Previously, in 1875, Parnell had been elected a Member of Parliament for County Meath for the Irish Parliamentary Party (Home Rule Party). The emphasis of the Party had now moved from repeal to Home Rule. There was, however, strong objection to Home Rule emanating principally from the north-east of Ireland, mainly from the Protestant population there, who considered that 'Home Rule would be Rome Rule'.

Although Parnell felt bound to follow a constitutional path, and indeed did so, there were times when his message was ambivalent on this point. In the USA he said in the course of one address:

> I am not in favour of revolutionary methods, yet still, as a sensible man, I cannot help saying that if things are allowed to continue as they are in Ireland much longer our people will not be able to content themselves or to withstand the influences which drive them towards violent and revolutionary methods.

In 1881 Parnell continued to be devoted to the pursuit of whatever form of Irish independence he could achieve. In the House of Commons he said: 'I have the greatest respect for many Fenians ... who believe in the separation of England from Ireland by physical force.'

However, he added, 'though I have this respect for these men I have never been able to see that physical force policy was practical or possible to adopt.'

Parnell was jailed for six months for 'being reasonably suspected of treasonable practices'. This arose from his opposition to the repression of the Land League and his support for tenants and for their 'no rent' campaign.

In 1886, eighty-six out of one hundred Irish members of Parliament were pledged to fight for Home Rule. In that same year, Gladstone introduced a Home Rule Bill, but it was defeated by a small majority. A second bill was proposed in 1890, but this coincided with a scandal involving Parnell, as a result of which the 'Uncrowned King of Ireland', as he was called, rapidly lost his 'crown'. Gladstone refused to have any further dealings with him.

The origin of the 'scandal' arose out of an encounter Parnell had in 1880 with Katharine O'Shea, the wife of Captain Willie O'Shea, a member of the Irish Parliamentary Party. Parnell was drawn to Katharine from the start, and she to him. Their relationship was covert, although it was considered that O'Shea was aware of it but took no action, because to do so before his wife came into a prospectively large inheritance would have been to his financial disadvantage. In 1883 Katharine gave birth to a baby girl (she already was mother to three children by her husband) and later to a further girl; Parnell was the father of both of these children. In May 1889, Katharine O'Shea's aunt died and she came into her inheritance. Divorce proceedings between Captain O'Shea and Katharine O'Shea followed, and Parnell's relationship with Mrs O'Shea then became public knowledge. The ensuing news resulted in a significant loss of support for the Irish Parliamentary Party. Parnell was now leader of a much reduced minority grouping.

The Catholic hierarchy in Ireland was now also against Parnell because of his affair with Mrs O'Shea. Parnell married Katharine on 25 June 1891. However, it was not long before his friends and adversaries noticed a marked deterioration in his appearance and it became obvious that his strength and health were failing. Katharine tried in vain to get him to see a specialist but he refused. He died from what was thought to be a coronary thrombosis on 6 October 1891. He was forty-five years old.

Parnell Monument, O'Connell Street/Parnell Square, Dublin.
Sculptor: Augustus Saint-Gaudens.

After Parnell's death, Gladstone introduced a further Home Rule Bill. This was passed by the House of Commons but was defeated in the House of Lords. Twenty years would pass before another similar act would be proposed.

Gaelic League
The ideals of the founders of the Gaelic League were similar to those of the literary side of the Young Irelanders. Douglas Hyde was one of the League's founders.

He was born on 17 January 1860 at Castlerea, County Roscommon. A Protestant, he was the third son of the Reverend Arthur Hyde and

Elizabeth Oldfield-Hyde. As a young boy, Hyde became fascinated with the Irish language. From this he also developed an intense interest in Irish folklore and history.

The League aimed at making the Irish language once again the spoken language of the people. Hyde complained in the following terms about the neglect of the Irish language:

> In fact I may venture to say that, up to the beginning of the present century, neither man, woman or child of the Gaelic race, either of high blood or low blood, existed in Ireland who did not either speak Irish or understand it. But within the last ninety years we have, with an unparalleled frivolity deliberately thrown away our birthright and Anglicised ourselves.

Ardent as he was in the fostering of the Irish language, Hyde wanted to keep the movement clear of politics, as although he agreed in principle with the aim of achieving freedom from Britain, he had grave doubts about the use of physical force. At an Ard Fheis (General Meeting) of the Gaelic League, held in 1915 in Dundalk, County Louth, the constitution was changed to include, in future, the realisation of 'a *free*, Gaelic speaking Ireland'. On the announcement of the vote favouring this, Hyde vacated the chair, left the meeting and relinquished his membership of the League forever. The growth of the League throughout Ireland continued (about 500 branches) and extended into England, Scotland and the USA. Referring to the meeting which set up the Gaelic League in the first instance, Patrick Pearse was later to say that it was the most revolutionary force that had ever come into Ireland and that the meeting provided 'the germ of all future Irish history'.

Douglas Hyde was elected the first President of Ireland in 1938.

Sinn Féin (Ourselves Alone) and the Irish Volunteers

The founder of Sinn Féin, Arthur Griffith, recommended that Irish Members of Parliament should refuse to attend the Parliament in

London and instead set up a council in Dublin to look after Irish interests. Griffith was prepared to accept that Ireland would remain in the British Empire under the King. By contrast, the majority of the members of Sinn Féin came to want what Wolfe Tone and the Fenians had wanted – an Irish Republic.

In 1912, Prime Minister Asquith's Home Rule Bill raised the ire of the Protestants of north-east Ireland in particular. They had up to now always relied on the House of Lords refusing any such bill; however, in 1911, a law had been introduced which provided that, in future, a bill passed by the House of Commons could not be 'vetoed' by the Lords, but merely delayed for two years. Meanwhile, the Unionists of Ulster, under the leadership of Dublin-born Sir Edward Carson (later Lord Carson), declared that if ever the Home Rule Bill were to come into law, they would rise in arms to prevent its implementation.

Consequently, by 1914, under the new law, the Bill would come into effect in due course, notwithstanding the opposition of the House of Lords to it. There were now in north-east Ireland over 80,000 Ulster Volunteers, armed and trained. They had drilled openly and had imported arms without hindrance by the British authorities. In the rest of Ireland, Nationalists, as a counter measure, now formed as the Irish Volunteers, and they felt, too, the need to arm themselves. This they endeavoured to do but, in this instance, they encountered determined British action to prevent it.

World War I, 1914–1918

In September 1914, Parliament decided that, because of the outbreak of war, the implementation of the Home Rule Bill would be delayed. This was much to the glee of the Unionists, and to the utter dismay of the Nationalists.

With the beginning of the war, Carson urged all his followers to instead use their arms against Germany. John Redmond, who had taken over the leadership of the Irish Parliamentary Party in Westminster following Parnell's death, gave the same advice to the Nationalists. However, most of those members of the Irish Volunteers who were also members of Sinn Féin refused to accept this on the basis that, until Ireland was free, they would not fight for another country. The Irish Volunteers were now split. The vast majority, now renamed the National Volunteers, followed Redmond's advice and many joined the British army. The minority, numbering about 10,000 (6%), regrouped.

The regrouping of what remained of the Irish Volunteers coincided with the creation of a unique body of young idealistic men and women. Incorporated in the grouping were members of the still-active IRB and Sinn Féin, together with supporters of socialist leader James Connolly.

Prominent among the activists were IRB members Bulmer Hobson, a Quaker from Belfast, and Leitrim man Seán Mac Diarmada (Mac Dermott). They published a newspaper entitled, unambiguously, *The Republic*. On moving to Dublin they joined forces with Sinn Féin. The grouping was totally opposed to Irishmen joining the British army. Their views on this can be illustrated by the following excerpt from *The Irish Review* of September/November 1914:

TWENTY PLAIN FACTS FOR IRISHMEN

- It is one thing to see the enemy's point of view: it is another thing to fight the enemy.
- The Irishman who says he would prefer to be under German rule than under English rule is a slave.
- The Irishman who says he would prefer to be under English rule than under German rule is a slave.
- The Irishman who knows he should be under Irish rule and under no other is capable of attaining freedom.
- The Belgian owes no allegiance to Germany.
- The Pole owes no allegiance to Russia, to Germany, or to Austria.
- The Irishman owes no allegiance to England.
- The organisation of the Irish Volunteers was begun on 25th of November, 1913.

○ The British Government, on the 4th of December, 1913, issued a proclamation prohibiting the importation of arms into Ireland.

○ Under the Arms Proclamation the British Government did what it could to hinder the Irish Volunteers from obtaining arms necessary to equip them for the defence of Ireland.

○ The Arms Proclamation was withdrawn in August, 1914, after the outbreak of an International European war.

○ Every foreign country from which the Irish Volunteers could have procured arms is now in a state of war or of neutrality.

○ Ireland, having no arms factory of her own, is thus still hindered from obtaining arms for her defence.

○ The Irish Volunteers have been organised first to secure the rights and liberties of all the people of Ireland, and then to maintain those rights and liberties.

○ The Irish Volunteers have not yet secured the rights and liberties of the Irish people.

○ The Irish Volunteers have no rights or liberties to defend.

○ The Irish Volunteers have not been enrolled to defend 'England and her Empire,' for the defence of which, according to the British proclamation, *Your King and Country Needs You,* the present war is being waged.

○ No body, committee or person, has any right or liberty to use or promise to use the efforts of the Irish Volunteers for any purpose other than the securing and the maintenance of the right and liberties of the people of Ireland.

○ The Union Jack is the symbol of the Act of Union of 1800, by which the Irish Nation was deprived of her last rights and liberties.

○ The Irish Nation lives.

THE PROTAGONISTS OF THE 1916 RISING

Patrick Pearse

Patrick Pearse in graduation garb. Image courtesy of the National Library of Ireland.

Patrick Pearse was born in Dublin on 10 November 1879. His father, James, a sculptor, was English; his mother was Irish. James set up business in 1877 in Great Brunswick Street (now Pearse Street), Dublin.

When Patrick was twenty-one years old he joined the Gaelic League. He became an active and enthusiastic member. His fluency in the Irish language qualified him to become editor of the League's newspaper, An Claidheamh Solais (The Sword of Light). He was driven to promote the language, too, because he feared that many people were becoming ashamed of using it. He was a barrister, a poet, a writer and an educationalist. He was also, in particular, a fervent Catholic. His plays, poems and stories were an indication of all that was dear to him: the natural beauty of Ireland, its people and their speech, especially the Irish language, and the country's history. All of these were underscored by his deep Christian convictions. Pearse founded St Enda's College in Dublin for boys, where the education of the pupils placed emphasis on Irish language, traditions and culture. He also established a combined girls' senior school and mixed preparatory school, named St Ita's, and appointed a Mrs Gertrude Bloomer as its headmistress.

A current image of the business premises of James Pearse and, below, a plaque on the upper level of the building showing portraits of Patrick and Willie Pearse.

SAINT ENDA'S COLLEGE

RATHFARNHAM

Headmaster - *P. H. PEARSE, B.A., Barrister-at-Law*

Apart from its Irish standpoint, ST. ENDA'S is distinguished from other secondary schools for boys by the appeal which its courses make to the imagination of its pupils, by its broad literary programme, its objection to cramming, its *viva voce* teaching of modern languages, and its homelike domestic arrangements which are in charge of ladies. The College stands on 50 acres of beautiful grounds. Recent successes include fifteen matriculations at N.U.I. A University Hostel is attached.

For Prospectus apply to the Headmaster.

Advertisement in 'The Irish Review', September /November 1914, for St Enda's College.

In the Gaelic League, Pearse met members who, like himself, came to realise that it would take more than education and the promotion of Irish culture to break the connection with England. His aim was to make a new Ireland 'not free merely, but Gaelic as well: not Gaelic merely, but free as well'.

He joined the IRB in July 1914, later becoming a member of the Supreme Council, and was heavily involved in the planning of the 1916 Rising. He and James Connolly were considered the primary leaders of it. His brother, Willie, also took part in the rising. Both Patrick and Willie were sentenced to death by execution for their actions, although those of Willie Pearse were of a relatively minor nature.

SALUTATION
George W. Russell (A.E.)
– Excerpt –

Here's to you, Pearse, your dream not mine,
But yet the thought, for this you fell,
Has turned life's water into wine.

Pearse's talent as an orator was illustrated on the occasion of the funeral of O'Donovan Rossa, who died on 29 June 1915 in St Vincent's Hospital on Staten Island, aged eighty-three. His remains were transferred to Dublin for burial and the occasion was a huge affair, garnering a substantial amount of publicity and support for the republican movement. Pearse's rousing graveside oration included the following words:

> Life springs from death, and from the graves of patriot men and women spring living nations ... they think that they have pacified Ireland. The fools, the fools, the fools! They have left us our Fenian dead, and while Ireland holds these graves, Ireland unfree shall never be at peace.

Funeral procession of the remains of O'Donovan Rossa, Dublin, 1915. Image courtesy of the National Library of Ireland.

James Connolly

In addition to Patrick Pearse, one of the prime movers of the 1916 Rising was James Connolly. Connolly was born on 5 June 1868 of Irish parents in Cowgate, then an Edinburgh slum. He received primary education at St Patrick's school, which was situated a few hundred yards from his birthplace. Poverty prohibited any further formal education and prospects of employment were meagre in the extreme. A way out of this impasse was to join the British army, and he did so in 1882. He was posted to Spike Island in County Cork and later transferred to Dublin. It was here that he met Lillie Reynolds, whom he later married in Scotland. He got a job as a carter and then took up a post in the Cleansing Department in Edinburgh. During his remaining six years in Edinburgh be became an active socialist and was fully involved in trade union affairs.

Statue of James Connolly. Located at a side entrance of the Custom House, facing Liberty Hall. Sculptor: Eamonn O'Doherty.

In 1896 Connolly returned to Ireland as a paid organiser of the Dublin Socialist Club; here he founded the *Workers Republic* newspaper. His reputation grew, and he undertook a lecture tour of the USA and Britain in 1902. His return to the USA in the following year resulted in his helping to found the Industrial Workers of the World Union. In 1910, he returned again to Ireland and became the Ulster organiser of the Irish Transport and General Workers Union (ITGWU), the union founded the previous year by his boss, James Larkin.

Mindful of the need to translate his socialistic beliefs through to the political sphere, Larkin, with James Connolly, founded the Irish Labour Party in 1912. Under the strong and charismatic leadership of Larkin, the membership of the ITGWU grew to about 10,000 within a couple of years.

By 1913, so many workers in Dublin had joined the union that employers became concerned and began to fire staff members who refused to relinquish their trade union membership. The employers took this action fearing that otherwise they might be forced to improve pay and working conditions, which in most cases were very poor. Under the leadership of businessman William Martin Murphy, about 400 business leaders combined to oppose trade unionism. A dispute with Murphy's Dublin United Tramway Company triggered the famous Dublin Strike/Lock-Out when over 20,000 workers, of various businesses, were sacked, including many who were not union members. The dispute lasted for about six months and resulted in huge hardship to the workers and their families. Fearing continuing damage to their businesses, however, the employers eventually agreed to accept unionised workers. This was the only gain for the workers, albeit a significant one, as the employees were forced to accept their employers' other conditions.

During the Lock-Out, Connolly had taken over the leadership of the workers when the then-leader James Larkin was arrested for convening a public protest meeting which had been prohibited by the authorities. In what became termed as 'Bloody Sunday', the police baton-charged those attending the meeting and scores were injured.

In 1914 Larkin left for the United States to organise workers in New York. He was not to return to Ireland until 1923.

The appalling suffering of the workers during the Lock-Out turned Connolly's mind towards political activity, and at the same time he organised the establishment of the Irish Citizen Army. He now considered that a physical strike against the British presence in Ireland was necessary and inevitable. He often quoted Camille Desmoulins, pamphleteer, journalist, and supporter of the French Revolution: 'The great appear great because we are on our knees. Let us rise.'

James Connolly's Irish Citizen Army outside Liberty Hall, Dublin, 1916. Image courtesy of The National Library of Ireland.

As a socialist, Connolly vehemently opposed the Great War. In it, he saw nothing but the continuing slaughter of working men from all countries in a conflict which netted gain only for the capitalists, while Ireland continued as an appendage to Britain, unable even to gain Home Rule for herself.

In the 1916 Rising, Connolly took part as military commander of the republican forces, which included his own citizen army. Before setting out to take over the General Post Office (GPO), he remarked quietly to a colleague:

'We are going to be slaughtered.'
'Is there no chance of success?' the colleague asked.
'None whatsoever,' Connolly reported cheerily.

The following Volunteers also took a leading role in the rising:

Thomas J. Clarke

Tom Clarke, born in March 1858 in England, spent almost sixteen years in jail in Britain because of his involvement in Fenian activities on English soil in the 1880s. He was confined under the most appalling conditions. The degree of torture applied to him and his colleagues, both mental and physical, resulted in many of them suffering from insanity.

On his release, he played a major part in the formation of the Irish Volunteers in 1913. He ran a newsagent's shop in Parnell Street in Dublin in which many IRB secret meetings were held. He fought alongside Pearse and Connolly in the GPO. He was the eldest and first of the leaders to be executed. He was fifty-nine years of age.

Seán Mac Diarmada

Born in County Leitrim, Mac Diarmada was a Sinn Féin organiser and in that capacity was well known all over the country. He was a close friend of Tom Clarke's. He became a member of the IRB and took part in the Howth gunrunning for the Irish Volunteers. He and Tom Clarke were side by side in the GPO. In his last letter to the Irish people he said:

The principles for which I give my life are so sacred, that I now walk to my death in the most calm and collected manner. I meet death for Ireland's sake as fearlessly as I have worked for the same cause all my life.

Thomas Mac Donagh

Thomas Mac Donagh hailed from Tipperary. He was a poet and a teacher and in the latter discipline he helped Pearse to found St Enda's College. He joined the Irish Volunteers in 1913 and the IRB in April 1915. In the rising, he was battalion commandant, located at Jacob's biscuit factory in Bishop's Street in Dublin. He wrote a long letter to his family on the night before his execution.

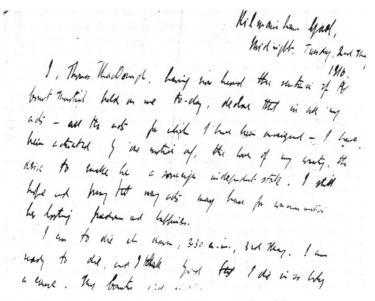

Part of Thomas Mac Donagh's original letter. Full transcript shown below.

Kilmainham Gaol
Midnight, Tuesday 2nd May
1916

I, Thomas Mac Donagh, having now heard the sentence of the Court Martial held on me today, declare that in all my acts – all the acts for which I have been arraigned – I have been actuated by one motive only. The love of my country, the desire to make her a sovereign independent state. I still hope and pray that my acts may have for consummation her lasting freedom and happiness.

I am to die at dawn, 3.30 a.m. ... 3rd May. I am ready to die, and I thank God that I die in so holy a cause. My country will reward my dust richly. ...

To my son, Don. My darling little boy, remember me kindly. Take my hope and purpose with my deed. For your sake and for the sake of your beloved mother and sister I would wish to live long, but you will recognise the thing I have done and see this as a consequence. I still think I have done a great thing for Ireland, and, with the defeat of her enemy, won the first step of her freedom. God bless you, my son.

My darling daughter, Barbara. God bless you. I loved you more than ever a child has been loved.

My dearest love, Muriel, thank you a million times for all that you have been to me. I have only one trouble in leaving life – leaving you so. Be sure, Darling, God will assist and bless you. Goodbye. Kiss my darlings for me. I send you the few things I have saved out of this war. Goodbye, my love, till we meet in heaven. I have a sure faith in our union there. I kiss this paper that goes to you.

I have just heard that they have not been able to reach you. Perhaps it is better so. Yet Father Aloysius is going to make another effort to do something. God help and sustain you, my love. But for your suffering this would be all joy and glory.

Your loving husband.

Thomas Mac Donagh

I return the darlings' photographs.

Good bye, my love.

Éamonn Ceannt

Born in County Galway, Éamonn Ceannt was employed as an account-ant with Dublin Corporation. He was a member of the Gaelic League and one of the founders of the Irish Volunteers. He was also a member of the IRB. As a member of the Military Committee of the IRB, he was engaged in the planning of the rising. During the rising, he was in charge of the 4th Battalion of the Volunteers stationed at the South Dublin Union and the Marrowbone Lane Distillery. Joint Second in command were Cathal Brugha and W.T. Cosgrave.

Joseph Mary Plunkett

Joseph Plunkett was born on 21 November 1887 in Dublin. His parents were quite wealthy. Unfortunately, Joseph contracted tuberculosis at a young age, and for this reason spent a part of his youth in the Mediterranean area and in North Africa. He developed a strong interest in Irish heritage and in the Irish language. A poet, he was a close friend of fellow poet Thomas Mac Donagh. He was a member of the Irish Volunteers and of the IRB. In his capacity as member of the latter movement he was asked to go to Germany in 1916 to liaise with Roger Casement, who was there in an effort to solicit aid from Germany for the rising.

Plunkett was intimately engaged in the planning of the rising. Just before the rising, his health deteriorated and he was hospitalised. He underwent an operation just days before Easter. Still weak and bandaged, he struggled to the GPO and provided as much help as he could. About seven hours before he was due to be executed, he married his sweetheart, Grace Gifford, in Kilmainham Gaol. In his book, *Down Dublin Streets*, Éamon Mac Thomáis described her position as: 'maiden, wife, widow – all in one day.'

THE STARS SANG IN GOD'S GARDEN
Joseph Mary Plunkett

The stars sang in God's Garden;
The stars are the birds of God;
The night-time is God's harvest,
Its fruits are the words of God.

God ploughed His fields at morning,
God sowed His seed at noon,
God reaped and gathered in His corn
With the rising of the moon.

The sun rose up at midnight,
The sun rose red as blood,
It showed the reaper, the dead Christ,
Upon His cross of wood.

For many live that one may die,
And one must die that many live–
The stars are silent in the sky
Lest my poor songs be fugitive.

Left: Door to the cell in Kilmainham Gaol, Dublin in which Plunkett was held and in which he married Grace Gifford. Right: Typical corridor in Kilmainham Gaol – cells on right-hand side.

Michael Mallin

Michael Mallin was born in Dublin in December of 1874. His father, John Mallin, was a carpenter. Michael joined the British army at the age of about fourteen. He served in India and Afghanistan and returned to Ireland at around the turn of the century. In Dublin he became a silk weaver and was appointed Secretary of the Silk Weavers' Union; he thereby became a close colleague of James Connolly, who appointed him commander-in-chief of the Irish Citizen Army. Following the surrender and while awaiting execution, he wrote a final letter to his wife, who was pregnant with their fifth child. The letter included the following words:

> My darling wife, pulse of my heart, this is the end of all things earthly; sentence of death has been passed and at a quarter to four tomorrow the sentence will be carried out and so must Irishmen pay for trying to make Ireland a free nation. I find no fault with the soldiers or police. I forgive them from the bottom of my heart ... Pray for all the souls who fell in this fight, Irish and English.

Countess Markievicz

Countess Markievicz was born Constance Gore-Booth in London on 14 February 1868. The Gore-Booths were an aristocratic and wealthy Protestant family from the west of Ireland. Unlike many of their class, the family was good to the tenants of their extensive estate both during the period of the Great Famine (1845–1849) and also subsequently whenever crops failed or were poor. The family home in County Sligo was named 'Lissadell'. Constance said of the surroundings:

> We lived on a beautiful, enchanted West Coast where we grew up intimate with the soft mists and the coloured mountains and where each morning you woke to the sound of the wild birds.

Constance Markievicz – humanitarian, actress, suffragette, freedom fighter, politician.
Sculptor: Séamas Murphy.

Constance and her sister Eva had many male admirers in Dublin and London society. They were immortalised by W.B. Yeats, a frequent visitor to their home in Sligo, in his poem entitled 'Lissadell'. In it he referred to the two girls as: 'two girls in silk kimonos, both beautiful, one a gazelle.'

In 1898 Constance moved to Paris to study art where, two years later, she married Count Casimir Markievicz from Poland. It is not absolutely clear what prompted Constance to turn her back on her comfortable background and, later, to embrace so fully the national-ist cause. However, it was said that, by chance, she came upon some back numbers of the Sinn Féin newspaper which contained articles on the life of Robert Emmet. So influenced was she about the down-trodden state of her own country that she immersed herself in doing whatever she could to put things right. It was this strong sense of justice that had already spurred her on to become a suffragette. She also became, under the influence of James Connolly, a strong socialist. Her concern for the poor was legendary. She worked tirelessly and selflessly, in particular for the poor of Dublin, by whom she was affec-tionately known as 'Madam'.

Constance joined Inghinidhe na hÉireann (Daughters of Ireland) which advocated militancy, separation from Britain and feminism. In 1909 she founded Na Fianna Éireann, a boy scout movement which disciplined boys as future soldiers and encouraged patriotism. She became a member of James Connolly's citizen army and took part in the 1916 Rising as second in command to Michael Mallin at Dublin's St Stephen's Green. She was sentenced to death for her part in the rising, but the sentence was commuted to life imprisonment because of her sex. She was released from prison in 1917.

Later, in 1918, while in jail for anti-conscription activities, Con-stance was elected as a Sinn Féin candidate to Westminster. She was in fact the first ever woman to be elected to the British House of Com-mons, but on her release she refused to take her seat as it would have involved both the swearing of an oath of allegiance to the King and recognising British jurisdiction in Ireland. She took her seat instead in the newly formed Dáil Éireann (Irish Parliament), where she was made Minister for Labour. She was the first woman anywhere in the world to hold such a government position.

Known for her involvement in putting on plays in Liberty Hall (trade union headquarters), she was asked on the day she was going to take part in the rising, by someone who had noticed a lot of activity, if the play was for children. 'No,' she replied, 'This one is for grown-ups.'

The O'Rahilly

Born in Ballylongford, County Kerry, O'Rahilly was a member of the Gaelic League and a founder member of the Irish Volunteers in 1913. He was not a member of the IRB and was opposed to the rising because of its timing, and his belief that, therefore, it could not succeed. Nevertheless, on his arrival at the General Post Office he was quoted as saying, 'Well, I've helped to wind up the clock, I might as well hear it strike.' On Friday, 28 April, and with the GPO now on fire, he volunteered to lead a small group of men to seek an escape route to a factory in Great Britain Street (now Parnell Street). He was shot and fatally wounded at the intersection of nearby Moore Street with Great Britain Street.

Éamon de Valera

Éamon de Valera was born in New York on 14 October 1882. His father, Vivian, died in 1885 and in that same year his mother, Kate de Valera (née Coll), originally from Bruree in County Limerick, decided that it would be best if Éamon were to be raised in Ireland. He was therefore brought to Ireland in 1885, where he was looked after by Kate's brother and his grandparents. When his schooling was complete, de Valera became a teacher. He joined the Gaelic League and, later, the Irish Volunteers.

De Valera joined the IRB somewhat reluctantly because he was wary of its being a secret society. Pearse appointed him a battalion commandant and in the rising he was in charge of a post at Boland's Bakery, defending three bridges and the railway route into Dublin's city centre. At his court marshal he was sentenced to execution. He received a reprieve, which some said was due to his holding an American passport. He himself maintained, however, that it was due to British misgivings arising from adverse public opinion being expressed about the number of executions already effected.

Éamon de Valera in uniform. Image courtesy of the National Library of Ireland.

Thomas Kent

The Kent family of Bownard House, Castlelyons, County Cork, was long associated with the struggle against British rule in Ireland. On 2 May 1916, just after the Easter Rising, their house was surrounded by a force of police and British troops who sought the arrest of the four Kent brothers. They refused to surrender. Their eighty-year-old mother played an active part in resisting their opponents, but they were eventually overpowered. One of the Kent brothers, Richard, was killed while trying to escape and Thomas Kent was arrested and later executed in Cork Jail.

Roger Casement

Roger David Casement was born on 1 September 1864 in Sandycove, County Dublin. His father, also named Roger, hailed from Ballycastle, County Antrim. He was a captain in the County Antrim Militia but resigned his commission due to his strong nationalist leanings, as he felt unable to take part in the eviction and destruction of the houses of the peasantry. He was a close associate of John Mitchell. Casement's mother was Anne Jephson, a Catholic from County Wexford.

Roger Casement. Original lithograph drawn on stone from life by Professor L. Fanto.

The young Roger Casement was educated in Ballymena. After spending two years working for a shipping company in Liverpool, he travelled in one of the company's ships to the west coast of Africa. Here he spent four years on an expedition which gained for him a high reputation as an explorer and an administrator. Following a number of British consular appointments, he was sent to the Belgian Congo to investigate rumours of 'mismanagement' by King Leopold of Belgium. He reported:

> There is so much to be done in the Congo matter that we shall need all our strength and the support of every friend of the weak and oppressed to help these poor wretched beings in Central Africa. It is a tyranny beyond conception – save only, perhaps, to an Irish mind alive to the horrors once daily enacted in this land.

And again, referring to the mutilation of human beings, he declared:

> It was not a native custom prior to the coming of the white man ... it was the deliberate act of the soldiers of the European administration, and these men never made any concealment that in committing these acts they were but obeying the positive orders of their superiors.

His report on the Congo received worldwide publicity and his work resulted in his being knighted. He now had an outstanding reputation for his humanitarian work.

In 1910 Casement was posted to Brazil with the task of sailing up the Amazon to Putumayo and to report on alleged atrocities on natives in the rubber plantations. Here he saw at first hand the exploitation of the natives which was being carried out on an immense scale. The 'white' agents were responsible for committing the most serious crimes, which included flogging, torture and murder. His efforts at bringing the atrocious conditions of the natives successfully to the fore had a detrimental affect on his health and in 1913 he retired. He devoted the remaining three years of his life to his own country.

All during his time in foreign climes, Casement kept in touch with what was happening in Ireland. In one of his letters he said: 'I have always said, as you know, that the Government would be beaten on Home Rule, and that even if they made the bill an act it would still never produce an Irish Parliament in being.'

Casement joined the Gaelic League and in July 1914 went to the USA to promote and raise money for the Volunteers. He was not a member of the IRB. In October 1914, Casement arrived in Berlin with the aim of obtaining arms from the German government and of forming an Irish Brigade from Irishmen who, having joined the British army, were now prisoners of war in Germany. In the latter matter he failed. However, after protracted efforts, he eventually succeeded in arranging a ship to sail to Ireland and to discharge a cargo of arms there, even though the amount of arms being shipped was much less than he had been hoping for. He travelled separately by U-Boat and, on 21 April 1916 (Good Friday), he landed on Banna Strand in County Kerry. He was captured there and taken via Dublin to London and placed in the Tower of London. Due to a misunderstanding, the agreed rendezvous for the landing of the arms failed to take place and the German ship, the *Aud*, was scuttled on the orders of her captain after it was captured by a British navy vessel and was being led to port. Casement was now convinced that, as he had failed to get the level of support he considered necessary from Germany, the rising should not be proceeded with.

Casement was convicted of high treason and sentenced to execution. Because of his extensive reputation for his humanitarian work, and because pleas for his sentence to be commuted began to be received, the authorities decided to start a whispering campaign to damage his character and reputation. This took the form of alleging that he was homosexual. As evidence for this, it was said that a set of diaries had been found in a trunk belonging to Casement in which references were made which indicated that he was guilty of illegal homosexual acts. The diaries were records of the atrocities Casement had encountered in Brazil. Casement was totally unaware of the allegations against him. Later, his defenders would allege that forged entries were made in the diaries. The matter remains contentious to the present day. One of the primary persons charged with the business of blackening Casement's character was Basil Thompson, head of the secret political police. In 1925, Thompson was convicted of an act of the grossest indecency in Hyde Park, London. In his defence in court, Thompson contended that he had written much on sexual crime, which he was studying. He retired to Paris where later he was found dead.

Excerpt from Casement's speech from the dock:

I assert from this dock that I am being tried here, not because it is just, but because it is unjust. Place me before a Jury of my countrymen, be it Protestant or Catholic, Unionist or Nationalist, Sinn Féineach or Orange, and I shall accept the verdict, and bow to the statute and all its penalties. But I shall accept no meaner finding against me than that of those whose loyalty I endangered by my example and to whom alone I made appeal. If they adjudge me guilty then guilty I am. It is not I who am afraid of their verdict – it is the Crown. If this is not so, why fear the test? I fear it not. I demand it as my right. This is the condemnation of English rule, of English-made law, of English government in Ireland, that it dare not rest on the will of the Irish people, but exists in defiance of their will; that it is a rule derived not from right, but from conquest. But conquest, my lord, gives no title; and, if it exists over the body, it fails over the mind. It can exert no empire over men's reason and judgement and affections; and it is from this law of conquest that I appeal. I would add that the generous expressions of sympathy extended to me from many quarters particularly from America, have touched me very much. In that country, as in my own, I am sure my motives are understood, and not misjudged – for the achievement of their liberty has been an abiding inspiration to Irishmen, and all men elsewhere, rightly struggling to be free.

Let me pass from myself and my own fate to a more pressing, as it is a far more urgent theme – not the fate on the individual Irishman who may have tried and failed, but the claims and the fate of the country that has not failed. Ireland has not failed. Ireland has outlived the failure of all her hopes – and she still hopes. Ireland has seen her sons – aye and her daughter, too! – suffer from generation to generation, always for the same cause, meeting always the same fate, and always at the hands of the same power. Still, always a fresh generation has passed on to withstand the same oppression. For if English authority be omnipotent – a power, as Mr Gladstone phrased it, that reaches to the very ends of the earth – Irish hope exceeds the dimensions of that power, excels its authority, and renews with each generation the claims of the last. The cause that begets this indomitable persistency, the faculty of preserving through centuries of misery the remembrance of lost liberty – this surely is the noblest cause ever man strove for, ever lived for, ever died for. If this be the cause I stand here today indicted for and convicted of sustaining, then I stand in a goodly company and a right noble succession.

Roger Casement was executed by hanging on 3 August 1916. His body was interred in the prison cemetery of Pentonville Prison. In 1965, his body was repatriated to Ireland where, after a State funeral, it was buried in Glasnevin Cemetery in Dublin. It was Casement's specific request the he be buried at Murlough Bay on the north Antrim coast. However, due to a condition laid down by the then British Prime Minister, Harold Wilson, that Casement's remains not be brought to Northern Ireland, Casement's wish was not adhered to. It still remains to be fulfilled.

THE VISION ON THE BRINK
Francis Ledwidge
– Excerpt –

Think of a long road in a valley low,
Think of a wanderer in the distance far,
Lost like a voice among the scattered hills.

And when the moon is gone and ocean spills
Its waters backward from the trysting bar,
And in the dark furrows of the night there tills
A jewelled plough, and many a falling star
Moves you to prayer, then will you think of me
On the long road that will not ever end.

Eoin Mac Neill

Born in County Antrim, Eoin Mac Neill was, with Douglas Hyde, one of the founders of the Gaelic League. He was also a founder of the Irish Volunteers and was their chief of staff. He was reluctantly in favour of a rising but, when it became known that the plan to provide arms from Germany had failed, he declared that he was no longer in favour of it going ahead. In fact, he issued in print a countermand order against the rising as late as Easter Sunday morning. This had the effect of causing major confusion, which resulted in the number of Volunteers ultimately taking part in the rising being only in the region of 1,000, compared with the anticipated number of about 3,000.

ACTION IN DUBLIN

On Easter Monday, 1916, the rising commenced. The principal focal point was the General Post Office (GPO) on Dublin's Sackville Street (now O'Connell Street). This was occupied by a combined force of Irish Volunteers and members of James Connolly's Irish Citizen Army. This location was supplemented by strategic outposts set up around the city. Patrick Pearse read out a proclamation outside the GPO.

POBLACHT NA H-ÉIREANN
The Provisional Government of the Irish Republic
TO THE PEOPLE OF IRELAND

IRISHMEN AND IRISHWOMEN: In the name of God and of the dead generations from which she receives her old tradition of nationhood, Ireland, through us, summons her children to her flag and strikes for her freedom.

Having organised and trained her manhood through her secret revolutionary organisation, the Irish Republican Brotherhood, and through her open military organisations, the Irish Volunteers and the Irish Citizen Army, having patiently perfected her discipline, having resolutely waited for the right moment to reveal itself, she now seizes the moment, and, supported by her exiled children in America and by gallant allies in Europe, but relying in the first on her own strength, she strikes in full confidence of victory.

We declare the right of the people of Ireland to the ownership of Ireland, and to the unfettered control of Irish destinies, to be sovereign and indefeasible. The long usurpation of that right by a foreign people and government has not extinguished the right, nor can it ever be extinguished except by the destruction of the Irish people. In every generation the Irish people have asserted their right to national freedom and sovereignty; six times during the past three hundred years they have asserted it in arms. Standing on that fundamental right and again asserting it in arms in the face of the world, we hereby proclaim the Irish Republic as a Sovereign Independent State, and we pledge our lives and the lives of our comrades-in-arms to the cause of its freedom, of its welfare, and of its exaltation among the nations.

The Irish Republic is entitled to, and hereby claims, the allegiance of every Irishman and Irishwoman. The Republic guarantees religious and civil liberty, equal rights and equal opportunities to all its citizens, and declares its resolve to pursue the happiness and prosperity of the whole nation and of all its parts, cherishing all the children of the nation equally, and oblivious of the differences carefully fostered by an alien government, which have divided a minority from the majority in the past.

Until our arms have brought the opportune moment for the establishment of a permanent National Government, rep-resentative of the whole people of Ireland and elected by the suffrages of all her men and women, the Provisional Government, hereby constituted, will administer the civil and military affairs of the Republic in trust for the people.

We place the cause of the Irish Republic under the protection of the Most High God, Whose blessing we invoke upon our arms, and we pray that no one who serves that cause will dishonour it by cowardice, inhumanity, or rapine. In this supreme hour the Irish nation must, by its valour and discipline and by the readiness of its children to sacrifice themselves for the common good, prove itself worthy of the august destiny to which it is called.

Signed on Behalf of the Provisional Government,

THOMAS J. CLARKE

SEAN MAC DIARMADA	THOMAS MAC DONAGH
P.H. PEARSE	ÉAMONN CEANNT
JAMES CONNOLLY	JOSEPH PLUNKETT

Dublin-born Seán Connolly (no relation of James Connolly) of the Irish Citizen Army led an attack on Dublin Castle, the bastion of British rule for well-nigh 800 years. Because of its size and the numerical strength of the Castle's occupants, Connolly's orders were to hold it at bay and not to attempt to capture it as a garrison. As it happened, probably for the first time ever, the Castle was almost bereft of soldiers as, apart from a handful, they were all on leave. Connolly was unaware of this and he and his small group took up positions in the neighbouring City Hall so as to have a good view of the Castle yards.

An urgent call went out for the British troops to return, and despite the best efforts of Connolly's group they were no match for the returning large force of British soldiers, which raked the City Hall and surrounding area with machine gun fire and hand grenades. By Tuesday morning the British were back in command of the area and Connolly and three of his colleagues were dead.

Dublin Castle, however, was still not free from attention by Republican forces. Thomas Mac Donagh and his company, in possession of Jacob's Biscuit Factory in Bishop's Street, had sight of the Castle. It took the British quite a few days to realise where fire was coming from, and during that time troop movements in the Castle's confines had to be stopped. When British troops did approach Bishop Street, they were forced back, having suffered a number of casualties. Second in command was Mayo native Major Séan Mac Bride, a veteran of the Second Boer War. Wexford man Michael O'Hanrahan also assisted Mac Donagh.

Meanwhile, Seán Heuston and his men took up positions in the Mendicity Institution, then situated near Ushers Island, and concentrated their fire on the nearby Royal Barracks (later named Collin's Barracks and now the location of the National Museum of Ireland). They had been asked to hold this position for three hours to stall the advance of British troops but managed to hang on for three days. At that stage their numbers, about thirty, were surrounded by five hundred British troops and Heuston decided to surrender. When he marched out of the garrison carrying a white flag, the British officers expressed amazement that they had been held at bay by a mere thirty Volunteers.

View of Heuston Station, Dublin, taken from Séan Heuston Bridge – both named in honour of Séan Heuston.

Under the command of Edward (Ned) Daly, Volunteer forces took up positions in the Four Courts and in eight other nearby locations. British troops poured into the area and easily isolated the separate Volunteer locations and put them under severe pressure. Finally, the Volunteers, having taken Linenhall Military Barracks (near the top of Capel Street), were forced to abandon it; but before being forced out, they set fire to it to prevent the British from re-entering. Daly's men also held Reilly's Fort – a strategically placed public house at the North King Street corner with Church Street – for almost eighteen hours.

On Easter Monday morning, Lieutenant Michael Malone and James Grace led a party of sixteen Volunteers to Mount Street Bridge in south Dublin. From various positions at and around the bridge, they attacked British soldiers making for Beggars Bush Barracks. British reinforcements numbering 2,000 landed at Kingstown (Dún Laoghaire). A contingent of somewhere between 500 and 1,000 of them made their way to the Mount Street area. In the ensuing encounters, sixteen Volunteers kept the British at bay for nine hours. In the end, four of the sixteen Volunteers were killed and the others were eventually captured.

The Fourth Battalion of the Volunteers under the command of Éamonn Ceannt had expected support of 1,000 men, but due to Mac Neill's countermanding order only about one hundred turned up. They took up positions in the South Dublin Union, Marrowbone Lane and Roes Distillery, Mount Brown (near Kilmainham). The greatly superior numbers of British troops eventually saturated these areas, forcing the rebels to move from one building to another. Nurse Keogh, while tending to a Volunteer who was wounded, was shot dead by a British soldier who mistakenly thought she was one of the rebels. Second in command, Cathal Brugha, was thought to have received as many as twenty-three bullet wounds when he was eventually captured by the British troops. He survived his injuries but was left somewhat disabled.

County Limerick-born Con Colbert, a member of the Irish Volunteers since its inception in 1913, was in command of the Ardee Street outpost of the South Dublin Union garrison before falling back to assist the Marrowbone Lane Distillery position. On surrender, he was arrested and later executed. He was twenty-eight years of age.

Based in St Stephen's Green, Commandant Michael Mallin of the Irish Citizen Army, supported by the Countess Markievicz, was reputed to have said, 'We would need 500 men to cover this area.' In the event, their full complement amounted to one hundred men and ten women. Outposts in nearby Earlsfort Terrace and Harcourt Street had to be abandoned because of this lack of Volunteers. Mallin did not have sufficient forces to attack the Shelbourne Hotel, and indeed when the British troops occupied it they had a free hand in concentrating their power on St Stephen's Green from the hotel's lofty rooftop positions. Having suffered many losses, Mallin and his forces later withdrew to the adjacent Royal College of Surgeons, which they continued to hold until the order to lay down arms was confirmed by James Connolly.

Royal College of Surgeons, St Stephen's Green, Dublin.

Usually in war situations innocent citizens also become victims; in this regard the 1916 Rising was no exception. One example of this was the killing of Francis Sheehy Skeffington, a journalist and classmate of James Joyce. He and two others, Thomas Dickson and Patrick Mc Intyre, were shot in Portobello Barracks by British soldiers. A commission of inquiry found that none of the three men was in any way connected with the rising. In fact, Sheehy Skeffington had been trying to prevent people from looting when he was arrested.

ACTION OUTSIDE DUBLIN

Kerry, Limerick and Clare

Due to Eoin Mac Neill's countermanding order, actions outside Dublin city were minimal. Volunteers in Kerry, Limerick and Clare were to have taken charge of the cargo of arms which was expected to be landed in Kerry by the German vessel, as arranged by Roger Casement. This did not come to pass.

Wexford

In Enniscorthy, County Wexford there was virtually no fighting because the British troops remained in their fortified barracks. Confusion caused by Eoin Mac Neill's countermanding order prompted Volunteer Paul Galligan to travel to the GPO in Dublin to seek clarification. Here he was instructed by James Connolly to return to Enniscorthy and hold the railway line to prevent troops coming through Wexford.

Meanwhile, the local Volunteers seized the whole town and held it until the surrender in Dublin was announced.

Galway

In County Galway, there were only a few engagements, headed by Liam Mellows, but they were relatively minor in nature.

Cork

When the news about the failed arms shipment was revealed, the Volunteers in Cork who had been preparing to travel to Kerry to pick up arms were unable to do anything but remain in Volunteer Hall in the city. British forces surrounded the hall and threatened that any movement of the Volunteers would result in the entire city being destroyed. After a week, the Volunteers surrendered and were arrested.

Meath

A large body of fully armed police was ambushed by the North Dublin Volunteers in Ashbourne, County Meath. The Volunteers were under the command of Kerryman Thomas Ashe, who was to die in 1917 as a result of force-feeding during a hunger strike in Mountjoy Jail in Dublin. Although the actions of the Volunteers against the Royal Irish Constabulary in Ashbourne were successful, they eventually had to comply with the order to lay down arms, as issued by Pearse in Dublin.

Laois

On Easter Sunday night, 23 April 1916, Laois Volunteers, under the direct order of Patrick Pearse, demolished a section of the Abbeyleix–Portlaoise railway line in order to prevent British forces reaching Dublin via Waterford after the commencement of the rising. This action took place at Coltwood. At approximately 9 p.m. a railway employee was seen inspecting the line, carrying a lamp. He was ordered by the Volunteers to halt but failed to do so. The local leader of the Volunteers, P.J. Ramsbottom, fired three shots at the man who extinguished his lamp and escaped in the darkness. Thus, it can be said that the first shots of the 1916 Rising were fired in County Laois.

Surrender

As the week passed, all Volunteer positions came under increasing pressure with the arrival in the city of more British troops from England, from the Curragh and other Irish locations. At the GPO, the first British arrivals, The Lancers, approached the building and suffered a number of losses. The British now brought heavier weaponry into play in the form of the gunship *The Helga*. From the River Liffey, she fired first on Liberty Hall and, later, on the GPO and surrounding buildings. At this stage, a large portion of Sackville Street was in ruins or on fire. James Connolly lay injured and exhaustion was affecting those who were not injured. With the GPO badly damaged and on fire, Pearse, Connolly and their men and women vacated the building and, still under fire, escaped to nearby Moore Street. When Pearse and Connolly saw the shooting down in the street of men, women and children who had been driven from their homes by the fires caused by the advancing enemy, and realising that they could do little more against the superior armoury of the British, it was decided that there was no option but to surrender. By the end of the week the rising was over.

Patrick Pearse was among the first to be executed for his part in the rising. The following poem was written for his mother and was included in his final writings in Kilmainham Gaol.

A MOTHER SPEAKS
P.H. Pearse

Dear Mary, that didst see thy first-born Son
Go forth to die amid the scorn of men
For whom He died,
Receive my first-born son into thy arms,
Who also hath gone out to die for men,
And keep him by thee till I come to him.
Dear Mary, I have shared thy sorrow,
And soon shall share thy joy.

1916 Rising. Damaged buildings in Dublin.
Image courtesy of The National Library of Ireland.

1916 Rising. Damaged buildings in Henry Street, Dublin. GPO on right. Image courtesy of the National Library of Ireland

The General Post Office, Dublin. Headquarters of the Rising – aftermath. Image courtesy of the National Library of Ireland.

Resulting from courts martial, the following were executed by British Firing Squad:

Wednesday, 3 May 1916
    Thomas Clarke
    P.H. Pearse
    Thomas Mac Donagh
Thursday, 4 May 1916
    Joseph Mary Plunkett
    Edward Daly
    Willie Pearse
    Michael O'Hanrahan
Friday, 5 May 1916
    Major John Mc Bride
Monday, 8 May 1916
    Con Colbert
    Seán Heuston
    Éamonn Ceannt
    Michael Mallin
Tuesday, 9 May 1916
    Thomas Kent
Friday 12 May 1916.
    James Connolly (Due to his severe injuries, Connolly was unable to stand for his execution and so was seated, strapped to a chair)
    Seán Mac Diarmada

Executed by Hanging:

3 August 1916 (London)
Roger Casement

Left: Stone Breakers Yard, Kilmainham Gaol. Site of execution of James Connolly. Location chosen due to proximity of gate, allowing easier entry for the badly injured Connolly. Right: Arbour Hill, Dublin. Burial place of the leaders of the 1916 Rising.

AFTERMATH OF THE RISING

In D. Casserly's book, entitled *History of Ireland* (1941), he summarises the impact of the 1916 Rising as follows:

> And so, the methods by which the government [British] had expected to put an end to Republicanism in Ireland had exactly the opposite effect, and Ireland, which until 1916 had known or cared very little about the ideals of Pearse and Connolly, were now more republican than she had been in the days of the United Irishmen and Wolfe Tone. The leaders of Easter Week, had achieved their object after all.

In hindsight, from a British perspective, the executions of the leaders of the rising and the deporting and imprisoning of those who escaped execution was a tactical error. The attitude of the general public, many of whom had been disinterested, dispirited and even hostile to the rising up to now, changed quickly to admiration, and the actions of the insurgents came to be seen by many as heroic.

In 1917, a number of by-elections were won by Sinn Féin candidates. A young man who had fought in the GPO now emerged on the scene to a significant degree. His name was Michael Collins. He was a member of the IRB, and a man who, it transpired, was gifted with great organisational and leadership skills.

Michael Collins. Image courtesy of the National Library of Ireland.

In this year too, de Valera came very much to the fore when he was elected unopposed as President of Sinn Féin, the organisation into which the Irish Volunteers now merged. In 1918 elections were held in which Sinn Féin made big gains.

	Before the Election	*After the Election*
Sinn Féin	7	73
Unionists	18	26
Irish Parliamentary Party & Others	78	6

As promised, Sinn Féin now confirmed their intention of not taking their seats in the Westminster Parliament and started to set up an independent Irish Parliament in Dublin – Ireland's first Dáil. The following appointments were made:

PRESIDENT OF THE DÁIL, Éamon de Valera
HOME AFFAIRS, Arthur Griffith
FINANCE, Michael Collins
DEFENCE, Cathal Brugha
FOREIGN AFFAIRS, Count Plunkett
INDUSTRY, Eoin Mac Neill
LABOUR, Countess Markievicz
LOCAL GOVERNMENT, W.T. Cosgrave
AGRICULTURE, Robert Barton

War of Independence
The threat to British rule in Ireland was not well received in Westminster, and it soon became evident that military conflict would ensue. It did so in January 1919 with an attack in Tipperary on members of the Royal Irish Constabulary (RIC) by Irish Volunteers. The Volunteers became known as the Irish Republican Army (IRA). The IRA was led by Michael Collins, whose spies in Dublin Castle provided him with valuable information. Great efforts were made by the British forces to capture Collins, but to no avail. In 1920, the British government, in response to the impact of the IRA, supplemented the RIC with a force of former soldiers which became known as the 'Black and Tans' due to the unusual assortment of uniforms worn by them. They were notorious in their indiscriminate and ruthless treatment of the IRA and their suspected sympathisers alike.

The guerrilla warfare was brutal and widespread. One of the fiercest incidents was when Collins, through his intelligence network, organised the killing of twelve undercover British Intelligence officers all on one day. Two auxiliary policemen were also killed. The British response was to send the Black and Tans into Croke Park, the Gaelic Athletic Association's principal sports grounds in Dublin. Here, a Gaelic football game was in progress, watched by a large crowd. They shot dead fourteen innocent civilians, including one player, and injured about sixty spectators. Later on that same evening, two high-ranking IRA officers, Dick Mc Kee and Peadar Clancy, were arrested and killed.

In that same year, 1920, the British government passed the Government of Ireland Act, under which they proposed the institution of two Home Rule states. One would be based in Dublin, covering twenty-six of the thirty-two counties of the country. The other would be based in Belfast and would comprise six of the nine counties of the province of Ulster. The six counties so chosen were those in which unionist opposition to Home Rule for Ireland had been strongest and in which, through gerrymandering, a unionist electoral majority would be guaranteed.

The intensity of the continuing War of Independence finally forced the British government to offer terms of a treaty. They were not to know that the IRA was then at virtual breaking point, due in no small part to their numerical disadvantage and to the dwindling stock of ammunition. The Republican forces numbered about 5,000 compared to the British forces of about 40,000.

In his capacity as President of the Irish Republic, de Valera sent a delegation, which included Michael Collins, to London to work out details of a treaty. The terms which were finally accepted by the delegation resulted in the partition of Ireland. Twenty-six counties would constitute 'The Irish Free State', and the six counties, north-east of where there would now be a border, were named 'Northern Ireland'. The Irish delegation had been under instructions to refer back any terms first to de Valera, but for reasons which remain unclear they failed to do so and instead signed the terms of the Treaty.

De Valera refused to accept the terms of the Treaty. The Dáil, however, ratified the Treaty by a majority of sixty-four to fifty-seven votes. With this, de Valera and his supporters resigned from the Dáil on 6 January 1922.

Arthur Griffith departing for London from Dún Laoghaire for the Treaty Conference. Image courtesy of The National Library of Ireland.

Troops of the National Army (Free State) replacing British Army troops at Richmond Barracks, Dublin, 1922. Image courtesy of The National Library of Ireland.

General Election

In a general election held in the Free State in June 1922, the electorate effectively accepted the Treaty by returning a majority of members who were in favour of it. There were fifty-eight pro-Treaty Sinn Féin members and thirty-five others (Labour, farmers and Independents) who were committed, to some extent, to accepting the Treaty. The anti-Treaty Sinn Féin members numbered thirty-six.

National Army (Free State) soldiers drawing up outside the Belfast Bank in College Green, Dublin, 1922. Image courtesy of University College Dublin Archives.

Civil War

A tragic civil war followed in which former colleagues in arms against the British now faced each other. The Free State government was led by W.T. Cosgrave on the pro-Treaty side. De Valera led the Republican side. In the midst of the fighting, devastating news affected both sides with the sudden death in August 1922 of Arthur Griffith, the founder of Sinn Féin, who was on the pro-Treaty side. A short while later, the shooting dead by Republican forces of Michael Collins, the leader of the Free State forces, was an even more devastating event.

An Emergency Powers Bill introduced by the Cosgrave government resulted in the execution of a number of Republican prisoners. The effect of these events was traumatic for both sides.

In May 1923, de Valera, backed by other Republican leaders, ordered the dumping of arms, thereby bringing the civil war to an end.

De Valera formed a new political party, Fianna Fáil, in 1926. His party first came to power, with the help of the Labour Party, following the general election of June 1932.

Michael Collins' cortège passing Government Buildings in Dublin. Image courtesy of the National Library of Ireland.

The Republic of Ireland

In September 1948, John A. Costello, the Taoiseach (Prime Minister) and leader of the Fine Gael party which emanated from the pro-Treaty side, stated his intention of declaring a republic. On 18 April 1949, the Republic of Ireland Act came into force and Ireland left the Commonwealth. She was now a fully independent state, albeit still a partitioned one, the north-eastern part, Northern Ireland, remaining a part of the United Kingdom.

REFERENCES

An Roinn Oideachais, *The Educational History of Ireland: Part II – from A.D. 1603 to modern times.* Dublin: The Educational Company (1959).

Berresford-Ellis, Peter, *The Boyne Water: The Battle of the Boyne, 1690.* Belfast: The Blackstaff Press (1976).

Bew, Paul, *Charles Stewart Parnell.* Gill and Macmillan (1980).

Boylan, Henry, *A Dictionary of Irish Biography.* Dublin: Gill and Macmillan (1988).

Byrne, Edward, *Parnell: A Memoir.* Dublin: The Lilliput Press (1991).

Casserly, D., *History of Ireland, Parts I and II.* Dublin: The Educational Company of Ireland (1941).

Chadwick, Nora, *The Celts.* Middlesex, England: Penguin Books (1979).

Chatterton Newman, Roger, *Brian Boru: King of Ireland,* Dublin: Anvil Books (1983).

Connolly, Colm, *The Illustrated Life of Michael Collins.* Boulder, Colorado: Roberts Rinehart Publishers (1996).

Cope, Joseph, *England and the 1641 Irish Rebellion.* Suffolk, UK: The Boydell Press (2009).

Cronin, Séan, *Wolfe Tone.* Dublin: The Sackville Press (1963).

Cullen, Luke, *Insurgent Wicklow: 1798.* Dublin: Clonmore & Reynolds Ltd (1948).

Cullen, Seamas, *The Emmet Rising in Kildare.* Dublin: Ifaelain Publications (2004).

Curtis, Edmund, *A History of Ireland.* London: Methuen & Co. Ltd (1936).

Demetrius, Charles Boulger, *Battle of the Boyne.* East Sussex: Naval and Military Press (2011).

De Nie, Michael Willem, *Studies in 1798 and 1848.* Fort Lauderdale, Florida: Dept of Liberal Arts, Nova Southeastern University (1999).

Dillon, Myles & Chadwick, Nora, The Celtic Realms. London: Sphere Books Ltd (1973).

Duffy, James, *Memoir of the Reign of Brian Boiroimhe, Monarch of Ireland*. Dublin: Published by the author (1843).

Duffy, Seán, *The Concise History of Ireland*. Dublin: Gill and Macmillan (2005).

Finlay, Rev. T.A. SJ., *With the Army of O'Neill*. Dublin: The Educational Company of Ireland (1930).

Fitzgerald, Rev. P., *Personal Recollection of the Insurrection at Ballingarry in July 1848*. Dublin: Fowler, 1861.

Fleming, Jim & Brendan, *1916 in Laois: An account of the activities of the Laois Volunteers up to and including the 1916 Rising*. Laois: Laois 1916 Commemoration Committee (1996).

French, Noel, *Battle of the Boyne 1690*. Meath: Trymme Press (1989).

Gilmore, George, *Labour and the Republican Movement*. Dublin: Republican Publications (1966).

Grattan, Henry, *Memoirs of the Life and Times of the Rt. Hon. Henry Grattan*. London: Colburn (1839).

Gwynn, Denis, *Smith O'Brien and Young Ireland*. Dublin: Irish Quarterly Review (1947).

Hayden, Mary & Moonan, George A., *A Short History of the Irish People, Part II*. Dublin: The Educational Company of Ireland (1960).

Hayes-McCoy, G.A., et al., *1798 Essays in Commemoration*. Dublin: Coiste Cuimhneacháin, 1798.

Hickson, Mary, *Ireland in the Seventeenth Century, Vol. I & II*. London: Longman Green & Co. (1884).

Higgins, Róisin & Uí Chollatáin, Regina, *The Life and After-life of P.H. Pearse*. Dublin: Irish Academic Press (2009).

Kee, Robert, *Ireland: A History*. London: Weidenfeld & Nicolson, 1981.

Kee, Robert, *The Laurel and the Ivy: The story of Charles Stewart Parnell and Irish nationalism*. London: Hamish Hamilton (1993).

Kenna, Kevin, *The Lives and Times of the Presidents of Ireland*. Dublin: The Liffey Press (2010).

Killanin, Lord; Duignan, Michael V.; Harbison, Peter, *The Shell Guide to Ireland*. London: Macmillan (1989).

Kostick, Conor & Collins, Lorcan, *The Easter Rising*. Dublin: O'Brien Press (2000).

Ledwidge, Francis, *Songs of the Field*. New York: Duffield & Company (1916).

Leonard, Hugh, *Parnell and the Englishwoman*. Harmondsworth: Penguin (1991).

Levenson, Samuel, *James Connolly: A Biography*. London: Martin, Brian and O'Keeffe (1973).

Little, W., Fowler, H.W., Coulson, J., Onions, C.T. (ed.), *The Shorter Oxford English Dictionary on Historical Principles*. London: Oxford University Press (1964).

Litton, Helen, *The Irish Famine*. Dublin: Wolfhound Press/Irish Books and Media (1994).

Mackey, Herbert O., *The Life and Times of Roger Casement*. Dublin: C.J. Fallon Ltd (1954).

Madden, Richard R., *The United Irishmen, their Lives and Times, Vol. II*. London: J Madden & Co. (1843).

Moore, Thomas, *The Life and Death of Lord Edward Fitzgerald*. New York: P.M. Haverty (1855).

Moloney, John Neylon, *A Soul Came Into Ireland: Thomas Davis, 1814–1845*. Dublin: Geography Publications (1995).

Murdoch, Henry, *My Killaloe*. Dublin: The Liffey Press (2014).

Mc Carthy, Denis Florence, *The Book of Irish Ballads*. Dublin: James Duffy and Co. (1869).

Mc Gettigan, Darren, *The Battle of Clontarf: Good Friday 1014*. Dublin: Four Courts Press (2013).

Mc Nally, Michael, *The Battle of Aughrim 1691*. Stroud, Gloucestershire: The History Press (2008).

Neill, Kenneth, *An Illustrated History of the Irish People*. Dublin: Gill and Macmillan (1979).

Norman, Diana, *Terrible Beauty: A Life of Constance Markievicz*. Dublin: Poolbeg Press (1991).

O'Boyle, Enda, *The Battle of the Boyne*. Meath: Duleek Historical Society (1990).

Ó Broin, Leon, *Robert Emmet*. Baile Atha Cliath: Sáirséal agus Dill (1954).

Ó Conchubhair, Pádraig, *The Fenians were Dreadful Men*. Cork: Mercier Press (2011).

O'Higgins, Brian, *Easter 1916: The Story of the Rising*. Dublin: Brian O'Higgins (1941).

Ó Máille, Eoin, *Roger Casement: The Forged Diaries Exposed*. Wicklow: M. Payne (1993).

O'Shea, Katharine, *Charles Stewart Parnell: His love story and political life*. London: Cassell and Company, Ltd (1914).

O'Donnell, Ruan, *Remember Emmet: images of the life and legacy of Robert Emmet*. Bray, Co. Wicklow: Wordwell in Association with the National Library of Ireland (2003).

O'Donnell, Ruan, *Robert Emmet and the Rising of 1803*. Dublin: The Irish Academic Press (2003).

O'Neill, Elizabeth, *Owen Roe O'Neill*. Dublin: The Talbot Press (1937).

O'Neill, H., *Memoir of Robert Emmet and the Irish insurrection of 1803; with the trial of Emmett for high treason, his memorable speech, etc.* London: Cleave (1840).

Reilly, Hugh, *Genuine History of Ireland*. Dublin: C.M. Warren (1837).

Scott, Brendan, *Culture and Society in Early Modern Breifne/Cavan*. Dublin: Four Courts Press (2009).

Shannon, J., 'Remembering RCIS and the 1916 Rising', *Irish Journal of Medical Science*, 175:2, pp. 5–9.

Somers, Dermot, *Endurance – Heroic Journeys in Ireland*. Dublin: The O'Brien Press (2005).

Sloan, Robert, *William Smith O'Brien and the Young Ireland Rebellion of 1848*. Dublin: Four Courts Press (2000).

Taylor, George, *History of the Rise, Progress, Cruelties and Suppression of the Rebellion in the County of Wexford in the Year 1798*. Dublin: William Curry Jun. & Co (1829).

Townsend, Charles, *The Republic*. London: Penguin Books (2014).

Wedgwood, C.V., *The King's Peace, 1637–1641*. London: William Collins & Sons & Co. Ltd (1955).

History Ireland, March/April 2014 Edition. Dublin.

The Irish Review, September/November 1914 Edition. Dublin.

The Spirit of the Nation, Dublin: James Duffy and Co. Ltd (1927).